Timothy Shay Arthur

Light on Shadowed Paths

Timothy Shay Arthur

Light on Shadowed Paths

ISBN/EAN: 9783337253530

Printed in Europe, USA, Canada, Australia, Japan

Cover: Foto ©Thomas Meinert / pixelio.de

More available books at **www.hansebooks.com**

LIGHT ON SHADOWED PATHS.

BY

T. S. ARTHUR.

Author of "*Ten Nights in a Bar Room,*" "*Steps towards Heaven,*"
"*What Can Woman Do,*" "*Golden Grains,*" *etc.*

NEW YORK:
CARLETON, PUBLISHER, 413 BROADWAY.
M DCCC LXIV.

Entered according to Act of Congress, in the year 1863, by
GEO. W. CARLETON,
In the Clerk's Office of the District Court of the Southern District of New York

CONTENTS.

I.	IF I COULD KNOW.	7
II.	BLUE SKY SOMEWHERE.	17
III.	LIGHT IN THE EVENING.	26
IV.	HE GIVETH HIS BELOVED SLEEP.	35
V.	IT IS WELL WITH THEM.	40
VI.	IF I HAD KNOWN OF THIS.	48
VII.	HE CAME IN MERCY.	58
VIII.	ONE DAY AT A TIME.	71
IX.	THE ANGEL-SISTER.	82
X.	OUR DAILY BREAD.	93
XI.	ALWAYS IN SUNSHINE.	101
XII.	MRS. GOLDSMITH AT FORTY.	112
XIII.	A DAY'S EXPERIENCE.	123
XIV.	JUST BEYOND.	133
XV.	MORE BLESSED TO GIVE.	142
XVI.	THE HELPING HAND.	148
XVII.	COMING DOWN.	157
XVIII.	THE POET'S LESSON.	173

XIX.	UP HIGHER.	185
XX.	WAS IT A MISFORTUNE?	197
XXI.	THE DEACON'S DREAM.	206
XXII.	WOULD YOU HAVE IT OTHERWISE?	216
XXIII.	IN THE HEREAFTER.	226
XXIV.	SHE WENT AWAY WITH THE ANGELS.	242
XXV.	THE WINE OF LIFE.	248
XXVI.	A POOR SERMON, AND WHY.	255
XXVII.	OLD GRIFFIN, THE USURER.	271
XXVIII.	A SPUR IN THE SIDE.	284
XXIX.	A NEW WORK AND A NEW LIFE.	295
XXX.	CARE-WORN.	310
XXXI.	SERVICE, NOT LOVE.	325
XXXII.	A RIFT IN THE CLOUD.	334
XXXIII.	SABLES.	341

LIGHT ON SHADOWED PATHS.

I.

IF I COULD KNOW.

HERMANN leaned back wearily from his study table, sighed, and sat in reverie for a long time.

"If I could only know that fruit would come of all this thought and effort," he said, breaking at length into the pause with speech. "If I could only know that the seed I am trying to scatter would fall into good ground."

He was silent again. Then a page in his Book of Memory was turned by an unseen hand, and he read from it this passage: "In the morning sow thy seed, and in the evening withhold not thine hand; for thou knowest not whether will prosper, either this or that, or whether they both shall be alike good."

He sighed once more, but the sigh was fainter. Then he bent to his work, writing slowly and with an intentness of thought that crowded the blood on his brain. These, among other sentences, came into existence:

"Of what did she die? The physician's certificate has it 'congestion of the brain.' But there be those who know better — those who, living in closer proximity, understand the case differently. Was the physician deceived? Possibly. Nay, certainly, for all his *post-mortem* examination. True, there was congestion of the brain, which, morbidly excited, took blood faster than it was able to use and return it; and this was the proximate cause of death — enough for the profession; but the real cause lay far away behind that, unrevealed to the eye of science. Of what, then, did she die? Simply of starvation! Nay, do not look incredulous, nor reject the assertion. It is true — sadly, sorrowfully true! She died, as thousands die daily around us, of starvation.

"You reject this, and with indignation. You knew her socially and intimately, were with her frequently during her last illness, and know that she took food daily, and in sufficient quantities to sustain life. But, for all this, our sweet friend died of starvation. There are those who live not by bread alone, who must have heart food or they can not live. Why are the cheeks of so many wives pale and wasted? The family physician, at fault, will look serious, and hint at organic derangement. He will recommend change of scene, exercise in the open air, more nutritious food — all merely professional, and not touching the case. If he could prescribe love!

"I saw, long ago, that she was failing. At first there crept over her pure face the thinnest veil of shadows. Something dreamy and pensive came into her eyes. She had a strange, earnest way of looking at her husband — tender, loving, but questioning. If she sat near him, or stood by his side, she leaned a little, as if drawn by an invisible attraction. I noticed, on his part, a cold irresponsive manner — a self-conciousness that held him away from all just perception of her states of feeling. His thoughts were busy in a world where she was not present. All the while she was asking for love, and looking for its signs in tenderly spoken words, in fond caresses, in kisses not coldly given, but burning with heart-fires. All the while she was hungering, and he kept back the full supply of food.

"Was he enstranged from her? Had love already died? Had she failed to reach his ideal of a wife? Not so. He loved her — as such self-absorbed men love their wives; was proud of her; looked into no woman's face and thought it sweeter than hers. She was making all his life pleasant, and he felt and acknowledged it with himself. But he was undemonstrative, as they say — did not express what he felt. Ah, that word undemonstrative, how often is it made to excuse mere indifference, or downright cold-heartedness! In fact, he was not worthy of such a wife, for he could not comprehend her nature, or, it may be, would not so rise out of his mere selfishness as to get a clearer vision. Be that as it may, he starved her by withholding the food her spirit craved with a never-dying hunger; and she paled and faded in his sight, wasting to ghostliness, and receding, until she passed the vale through which none return — passed, as many wives pass, year by year, killed by the same disease.

"O man, consider and be wise, ere the days of darkness come, when it will be too late! Is there a pale face in your home? Do loving eyes look at you in wistful sadness from sunken orbits? Are you in daily fear that a blast falling down suddenly will sweep to the other side the spirit-like form which, once absent from your dwelling, will leave all its chambers desolate? So far the physician has failed. Medicine does not reach the disease. Sea-bathing, mountain air, mineral springs — all have been tried, and still the white face grows whiter, the shrinking form more and more attenuate, the eyes sadder, the spirits more depressed. You have done and are still doing all in human power to save her. No — something yet remains! Try loving words and deeds.

Lay your hand, as of old, tenderly on her head; smooth the hair with soft caresses; look down, with the look that blessed her years ago, into her dimming eyes, and let them take a new lustre from your own; tell her that you love her, for this will do her good; she is hungering for the words — has hungered for them, oh so long and so wearily! until faint with waiting. Give her the food for lack of which she has been dying daily for years. O man! again I say be wise, ere the days of darkness come, when it will be too late."

Hermann paused, laid down his pen, and leaned back from the table.

"If I could have said all that was in my thought; but language is so inadequate! The ideas that throng my mind lose half their clearness when I attempt to express them. Ah, if I knew that even this poor work would not die — that it would save one life failing for lack of love."

Another leaf in his Book of Memory was turned by an unseen hand, and on it was written: "Cast thy bread upon the waters; for thou shalt find it after many days."

"Let it go forth," he said, in a more cheerful voice, rising from the table. "If the seed is good it will fall into good ground somewhere. Man soweth, but with God is the increase."

It went forth; and, like all good seed cast from the

sower's hand, fell by the wayside, on stony places, among thorns, and also into good ground. God knew of the increase, if Hermann did not. It was a part of *his* discipline to have faith and patience.

A month or a year have passed. It matters not. Truth never dies; never loses its vitalizing force. Sitting alone, with a troubled countenance, was a man scarcely yet touching the meridian of life. A periodical which had engaged his attention lay half-closed on the table beside him. The trouble in his face was mingled with surprise, as though he had just received a painful revelation.

"Starved to death!" There was a shiver in his voice. "Is that indeed possible?"

Even as he said this, the door opened and a woman came in, with almost noiseless feet gliding slowly across the apartment. Her face had the exhaustion and pallor that long sickness leaves behind, and was veiled by a touching sadness. She did not look toward the man but his eyes followed her as she moved about the room with an expression of deep and yearning interest. After obtaining what she sought, the woman — still without seeming to be conscious of the man's presence — retired to the door through which she had entered, and was passing out, when the man, speaking with suppressed feeling, said,

"Florence!"

There was evidence of surprise in the woman's manner as she paused and half-turned herself, now for the first time looking at him.

"Florence, you are very pale to-night." The voice was not steady.

What a strange, startled look came into the woman's face!

"Come!" He spoke tenderly, and held forth one hand in invitation. "Come, dear!"

The woman moved away from the door, crossing the room toward him, her eyes fixed searchingly on his countenance. There was a shade of doubt in her manner.

"Sit down." He moved a chair close to the one he occupied, but a little in front, so that he could look at her directly, and, taking her hand as she approached, drew her down into it. Still holding her hand after she was seated, and still gazing at her with eyes full of interest, he said:

"Are you not so well to-night, Florence? You look unusually pale."

Her cheeks found, on the instant, unwonted color. Her eyes shone with the flushing of tears. There was a motion of her lips, but no words parted them.

"It hurts me, darling, to see you drooping about in

this sad, weary way. Can nothing be done? Have you pain to night?"

The tenderness of voice was genuine. The man's heart was stirring from a long, dull sleep — and it was time.

"I have no pain." She bent forward quickly and hid her face against him, catching her breath and holding back a sob that was leaping past her throat.

With a touch that sent a thrill of joy along every awakening nerve, the man laid his hand upon her head, smoothing back the hair with soft caresses, then stooping over, he kissed her.

"What does this mean, Harvey?" The woman lifted herself all trembling, and drawing back, looked in a wild, eager way into her husband's face.

"What can it mean, Florence, but love? Are you not my pure, true-hearted wife? Oh that I could bring back the old light to your eyes, the old health to your cheeks, the old gladness to your heart! What can I do, Florence?"

"Love me as of old," she answered, passionately, flinging herself on his bosom. "Oh, my husband! I am starving for lack of love."

"Not starving, Florence! Oh, my wife! how can you say this when you are the most precious thing I have in this world? When the fear of losing you forever haunts me day and night?"

She raised herself again. As her face became visible her husband saw that it was almost radiant. The lost sweetness and beauty were restored.

"Am I awake or dreaming?" she said.

"You are awake, dear — wide awake, after a long nightmare," was answered.

"Perhaps I may sleep again." Her voice fell.

"Not if in my power to hold you away from enchanted ground. I may have seemed cold on the outside, Florence, but my heart was warm. It carries no image but yours. Trust me, for the future."

"Our lives, Harvey, touch the outside of things," she answered; "and if that be cold, how can we help feeling the chill? If there is no tenderness in the eyes and voice, if loving speech is withheld, how can we be sure that love is in the heart? There may be rain enough in the clouds, but if it fall not on the thirsty flowers they will perish. Don't forget this, Harvey; and if you love me say the sweet words often, that my soul may have assurances and joy."

If Hermann could have looked on this scene he would have known what kind of harvests ripened from seed he was scattering — in doubt and hope — broadcast among the people, wearied often, and sometimes fainting. But he could not know. And it was as well. Self-discipline and strife with doubt were needed for the perfecting of his life. The unrest, born of vague questionings as to use and duty, gave vitality to thought, quickened his mind for higher efforts, and held him to work that needed to be done. And it was a good work if such fruit as we have seen crowned many of its harvests. Faint not, Hermann! "In the morning sow thy seed, and in the evening withhold not thy hand; for thou knowest not whether will prosper, either this or that, or whether they both shall be alike good."

II.

BLUE SKY SOMEWHERE.

IT was the remark of a child, consoling himself for the loss of a promised pleasure on a rainy afternoon, that there was "blue sky somewhere." And the sapphire heavens, flooded with sunshine, on the next day made his faith a verity.

The lesson is for you, and for all of us, reader; and we need it quite as much as the boy who sat looking out of the window upon a leaden sky and the fast-falling rain, and trying to find comfort in the thought that, far above the cloud and storm, the sun was shining in his undimmed splendor.

"Into each life some rain must fall," says the poet-teacher; and in the days that come "dark and dreary" we are apt to feel, in spite of experience and reason, that the brightness has passed from our lives forever. But it is not so. Like travelers we rise, now upon mountain heights, and now descend into deeply shaded valleys; pass through open savannas, down upon which the golden sunbeams fall; and anon are buried in dense forests, that seem stretching their interminable vistas to the very end of our journey. We encounter all aspects of the heavens; have our mornings, our noondays, our evenings, and our nights with only the stars for guidance; our wild, contending storms, and our sunny, tranquil atmospheres. Has it not been so with you, reader? And yet, when the sun goes down, or hides his face in mantling clouds, does not your heart grow faint, and your faith in " blue sky somewhere " become feeble as the rays of an expiring lamp? The very children are our teachers!

Between our inner and our outer worlds there is something more than simple analogy; the relation bears the higher one of correspondence, even to minutest things; so that nature, with all its infinite varieties of aspects and changes, representing interior aspects and changes, becomes our instructor. Our true poets rise into a perception of this, and give us lessons of wisdom that sink deeply into the heart, and become to us as lights in dim places, strength in weariness, and confidence in last results when the mind is trembling in doubt and fear. Not mere words in rhythmic order are the poet's, when he says:

> "Be still, sad heart! and cease repining;
> Behind the clouds is the sun still shining;
> Thy fate is the common fate of all,
> Into each life some rain must fall,
>   Some days must be dark and dreary."

"If I could only believe that the clouds would pass away — that sunny days would come again — I might weep less," was the language of one who sat in the darkness of sorrow and disappointment, as a friend and consoler offered her the poet's lesson, that she might take it into her heart. "But I can see no rift in the clouds; no line of light along the dark horizon; no abatement of the fast-falling rain."

"We are sure that the rain will cease; that behind the clouds the sun is shining. We have the fullest confidence in returning sunbeams; and why? Because we know that clouds are merely earthly exhalations; that they do not rise high in the heavens — that they can never reach the sun, whose beams shine ever on with undiminished splendor, and have power to disperse the densest vapors that ever drew their curtains before his radiant face. Now the world of mind, like the world of nature, has its sun, as the poet has so beautifully intimated. Thought sees by its light, and the heart is refreshed and beautified with flowers and verdure by its warmth. But at times this sun is hidden by clouds, and there are shadows in the mind and rain upon the heart. The days are dark and dreary. Why? Whence are these clouds? Let visible things become our teachers."

The countenance of the listener grew attentive, and the friend went on:

"They go up from the natural earth, as clouds go up from the earth of our minds; and even while we sit in sorrow for the beams that have faded from our paths, the sun is dissolving these clouds in rain for refreshment and fruitfulness. Our hearts are watered in the days of sorrow, that they may bear good fruit when the sunshine comes again."

"If it ever comes." The despondent soul could not look beyond the clouds.

"Have you heard of Mrs. Elford's trouble?" asked the friend.

"No." There was a quick flash of interest in the mournful face. "What of her?"

"Her husband is dead."

"Oh no!" The lady clasped her hands in sudden surprise and pain at this intelligence.

"The news came yesterday. He died on the Pacific coast."

"Captain Elford?"

"Yes."

"Oh dear! that is trouble! And he has left her poor, without doubt."

"I fear as much."

"Have you seen her?"

"Yes, I called this morning."

"How is she?"

"Entirely prostrated by the blow."

"Poor Margaret!" The tone of sympathy was genuine. "I must go to her in this affliction. I must try to speak some word of comfort."

"She needs all the support her friends can give. It is her hour of darkness, and she is sorrowing as one without hope. The sun has withdrawn himself behind thick clouds, which are pouring down heavy rain upon her life. Yes, go to her by all means, and tell her that, though her sky is dark to-day, and filled with cloud and storm, that the sun of God's love is still shining as brightly as ever, and will, in the good time of Him who is all-merciful, send down his beams upon her heart again."

It was an old and dear friend who had passed under the cloud of sorrow, and the doubting and despondent one, already half-forgetting her own pain, was pondering over words of consolation.

"God is really nearer to us in affliction," she said, as she sat holding the nerveless hand of Mrs. Elford, "than at any other time, though He may seem farthest off; for His infinite, divine pity, is moved with the tenderest compassion for the griefs of His children. Though His face may be hidden from us, it is not the less a smiling face."

A sob and a long tremulous sigh were the only answer.

> "Into each life some rain must fall,
> Some days must be dark and dreary."

Yet no response came. The words of the comforter seemed as if spoken to shut ears. Not so, however. They entered, and like seed when first cast into the ground, gave no life-sign of their presence. But memory held them for the time of fructification.

And now it happened to the despondent and grieving one, who had refused to be comforted, yet tried to speak in consolation to another heart, that light seemed to come around her. She did not see the sun, nor even a rift in the clouds with azure in the far distance. But it was not so dark in the chambers of her soul. The pressure on her spirit that seemed at one time as if it would close her life in suffocation, was not so great. She could breathe deeper, and with even a sense of relief and satisfaction.

"My poor friend!" she said, many times, as she thought of Mrs. Elford. And as her desire to bring relief to another heart grew stronger and stronger, her own consciousness of suffering diminished. In the magnitude of another's sorrow, hers seemed to grow less.

Almost daily she visited her afflicted friend, into whose sad face a little light would come on her appearance; and though it faded instantly, the sign of pleasure at seeing a welcome countenance was too palpable for any mistake as to its origin. She had really been helped and comforted, though she knew it not; and the face of the comforter was therefore welcome.

When next her own friendly visitor called, she was not sitting in idleness, brooding over the irrevocable past; but really forgetful of the past in present thought of home duties with which her hands were busy.

"How is it with you to-day?" said the friend, as she took her hand. "But I need scarcely ask, for the cheerful tone of your countenance tells me that light is breaking through the clouds."

"I have been too busy to think dark thoughts this morning," was the answer; and even as this was said the lips which had arched with a feeble smile fell back into a sadder outline.

"Busy in what?"

"In the duties of my home. I'm afraid that, under the pressure of pain, I grew selfish, loving to nurse despondent states, and growing forgetful of the comfort and happiness of those around me. And now I am trying to make amends."

"And in the first right effort comes a more peaceful state."

"Perhaps so."

"Don't speak doubtfully. Say yes."

"I am not so much depressed in mind as I have been."

"And if you keep on in this path of duty the weight which has been bearing you down will grow less and less burdensome; the clouds that mantle your sky thinner and thinner, until light breaks through, and disperses them altogether. There are only some dark days in our lives, and the sun must and will penetrate the gloomy vapors, and reveal his smiling countenance. If these days are prolonged it is our own fault. But how is Mrs. Elford? I have not seen her for some time."

"More cheerful," was the answer.

"That is gratifying."

"She received a few days since a long and satisfactory letter — if I may use the the word satisfactory in such a connection — about her husband, who had the most careful attendance and every comfort during his last illness. Unexpectedly, this letter brought her the intelligence that Captain Elford left property to the value of nearly fifteen thousand dollars, the result of some trading adventures on the coast."

"Then she is not left destitute?"

"No."

"Already there is a break in the clouds, showing a clear blue sky above them."

"Yes."

"And the days must come for her as well as for you, and for all whose sky has become dark and threatening, when the broad, bright sunbeams will flood the whole horizon again. Let us not give away to weak distrust, or a paralyzing despondency, when the rainy days come: but keep hands and thought busy with useful work, having faith in the law that governs the world of mind as well as the world of nature, and live in hope of to-morrow's sunshine. What is the lesson past experience teaches? Is it not the same in regard to the inner as to the outer world? There have been times of cloud and rain, and times of sunshine. There have been declining days, even to evening and solemn night; and mornings coming in beauty and joy. Even the seasons are represented in our varying states of mind, as the years progress toward a completion of their earthy cycle. And all these changes are for the sake of fruit — the fruit of righteousness. Let us be mindful, my friend, of the lesson, and not keep too much out of the sunshine; lest, when we come to make up our sheaves in the harvest-time, there be found only husk instead of grain."

III.

LIGHT IN THE EVENING.

"THE days grow darker and drearier as we get older." This came from one of two friends, whose years had fallen into the "yellow leaf."

"But, there shall be light at evening," said the other, in a cheery voice.

"Not unless the order of nature be reversed, Mr. Fairfax," was replied. "When the sun sets, day goes out in darkness."

"And yet, for all this, friend Ascot, there will be light at evening. Not half so dark as feared, will the shadows fall; and, quickly, shall the east grow radiant again. Has it not always been so? Have we not always found light at evening, instead of the famed Egyptian blackness. Take your own experience. Think back over the dark days through which you have passed and to the close of which you looked with a shudder. Did not light come at evening? The sun broke through lifting clouds; or, day came suddenly in the east — a purer, calmer day than any you had ever known."

"I often wish that I could see with your eyes, Mr. Fairfax," replied the friend. "But my natural temperament is different. I am apt to look on the gloomy side of things; to turn my back to the light."

"Of course, if we turn ourselves from the light, we cannot receive its blessing. And yet, sitting down, of our own choice, among shadows, we complain that the days grow darker and drearier as we get older."

The door of the room where the two old men were sitting opened, and a young woman entered with a tray in her hand, on which were two saucers of ripe strawberries. She set them down on a table, saying, with a smile:

"They are just from the garden. I thought you would enjoy them."

"Light in the evening!" Mr. Fairfax looked at his friend, as the young woman went out. Dropping his eyes to the floor, Mr. Ascot mused for a little while, then said, partly speaking to himself:

"Yes, it is lighter than I anticipated. I thought this day, in the days of my life, would go down in the very blackness of darkness. I was angry with my wayward son, when he took him a wife, because I fancied he had stooped in marriage. He had never been much comfort to me before that time, and I gave up all hope in him for the future. But there was a good providence in the event, which I did not then see. Even while I was drawing around me the curtains of doubt and gloom, her hand was moving among the overhanging clouds, and bearing some of their heaviest folds aside. To my son she proved a good angel. He loved her, and she was worthy of his love. You know that he died. I did not, at first, feel like receiving the widow home. There were no children, and I said to myself, 'She is nothing to me now. Why should I take up the burden of her support? Let her go back among her friends.' Partly to satisfy public sentiment, and partly because her pure and loving nature had begun to influence me, I took her home. It was the closing of a day of sorrow and disappointment, and yet I say it thankfully, at the evening time there was light. No daughter could be more loving or more thoughtful of every comfort. What should I do without her?"

"Yet only a little while ago you complained that, as years increased, the days grew darker," said Mr. Fairfax.

"And so I find them." Mr. Ascot's countenance, which had brightened while he spoke of his daughter-in-law, fell again. "There may be a little gleam here and there — a struggling of light, in feeble rays, through broken spaces — but, I see over all things a steadily increasing gloom."

"From whence does it come, my friend? This gloom is an effect. Do you see the cause?"

"The causes are manifold. Everywhere disappointment tracks my path. The full promise of spring has never come in the summer-time, nor the promise of summer at fruit gathering. Always, realization falls below the hope. So it has ever been with me, my friend; until now I have lost all confidence in the future; have ceased to look for any good.

"And yet," said Mr. Fairfax, "even while you are thus complaining, good gifts are showered upon you in rich abundance."

"I should like to see them," answered Mr. Ascot, half amused, yet with a flavor of irony in his voice.

"Sometimes there is obscurity of vision. The objects exist, but we do not perceive them. I think it is so in your case."

"Ah?" with a faint, incredulous smile.

"Take your natural life," said Mr. Fairfax. "What is lacking to your enjoyment?"

"O dear! almost every thing," was impulsively answered.

"What? Is there lack of pleasant food, or refreshing drink, or soft and warm clothing, for the body? Have you not all things in liberal abundance? Is any thing desired for comfort absent from your dwelling? or, does an enemy threaten to despoil you?"

Mr. Ascot shook his head. "I have nothing to complain of in this respect. "But——" He paused, grew thoughtful, and remained silent.

"Yet, for all this, your heart is troubled. There is on your mind a weight of dissatisfaction — you feel a constant yearning after something not clearly seen; the nature of which is not clearly apprehended. Your days are not sunshiny, and you feel, as the evening draws on, that it will go down in clouds."

"Yes. You state the case exactly."

"And still I say," Mr. Fairfax spoke cheerily again, "that there will be light in the evening. Always, even in the most external events of your life, when the period of trial, or sorrow, or misfortune closed — when the day's dreaded termination came — light poured in from the west through rending clouds, on the day of a new and higher state, broke in the purpling east. The instance to which you a little while ago referred is but one of hundreds that stand recorded in your memory, if you will open the book and read. But, for you and for me, my friend, there is a day going down, toward the evening of which thought cannot fail often to look forward. Shall there be light then? Will the last setting of our sun leave us in darkness; or shall it be only the herald of a day-spring from on high?"

"You have touched the key note of a depressing theme," was answered. "Some men turn from the idea of death stoically, and some with indifference, while others contemplate the event serenely, and see in it only a brief passage to heaven. Not so with me. The thought of this last time comes always in gloom. I turn from it in depression — sometimes with a shudder."

"And yet you are a church-member."

"Yes."

"And have, I think, tried earnestly to keep the divine law."

"As far as I understand the commands of God, I have tried to live up to them. The time was when I did not give much heed to this law; but, for many years past, I have not wilfully gone counter to its clear enunciations."

"'If ye love me, keep my commandments. If ye continue in my Word, then are ye my disciples indeed. What more than this?'" The friend spoke in a low, impressive voice. "If we obey the divine law, sincerely; that is, because it *is* the divine law, and not because we may have wordly gain as nominal Christians, we need have no fear of the last time. Death will come as a gentle spirit, and taking us by the hand, lead us through the valley. There will be light at evening, though the declining day be veiled with clouds."

Sooner than either of the friends had imagined, this prophecy was closed. A year had not passed, when Mr. Fairfax learned, one day, that Mr. Ascot was sick. He found the daughter-in-law in tears.

"Not seriously ill, I trust," he said.

"We have very little hope of him," was answered in a voice choked by sobs. "He seems to be failing rapidly."

"I am pained to hear this," said Mr. Fairfax. "How long has he been sick?"

"For some months I had thought him failing; but he made no complaint. Three weeks ago he became suddenly ill, and has been rapidly going down ever since."

"What about his state of mind?"

"He is very calm."

Mr. Fairfax went up to the sick chamber. On the face of his old friend he saw death written; not in fearful lines, but in radiant characters. A smile broke over the pale features, lighting them up as if a curtain had just been drawn aside, admitting the sunshine. The hands of the two old men were laid within each other, and tightened.

"I did not, until now, hear of your illness," said Mr. Fairfax, " or I would have seen you before."

"It has been severe, breaking me down rapidly," was feebly answered. Then, after a brief pause, he added — "The evening about which we talked, one day not long ago, has come."

"That evening which comes, soon or late to all."

"Yes."

"And is there light?"

"There is light, my friend. For a little while it seemed as if the day would go down in blackness; but angel hands soon commenced folding back the cloudy curtains that shut away the sun-illumined sky, and now, instead of darkness, there is light. Instead of sun-set, it is sun-rising. Even as I trembled at the approaching shadow, a sweet voice cried to me, 'Lo, the morning breaketh!'"

"And all fear is gone?"

"What is there to fear?" feebly answered the sick man. "God is just and merciful. He knows what we are; how much we have been tempted; and how sincerely we have tried to keep His law. He is a discerner of the thoughts and intentions. Our purpose to do right, even though we have often failed of right action, will be the witness in our favor. Here, confidently, I rest my case, and tranquilly await my Lord's decision."

"Actions are really good only in the degree that they have the inspiration of a good purpose," said Mr. Fairfax. "Only such actions find favor with God. So, resting in confidence on your will to do right, you look for the joyful words — 'Well done!'"

Mr. Ascot closed his eyes and lay still for some time. The look of heavenly peace did not fade from his countenance. Presently the eyes opened again, but their expression was new. They saw, but not the fixed and circumscribed objects in the death chamber. There had been granted a clearer vision — mortal investures were folded away. The lips moved, as the face grew bright. Mr. Fairfax bent to hear:

"It shall come to pass — that — at evening time — it shall be light."

"God's promise fulfilled," whispered Mr. Fairfax. "The evening has come, and it is light!"

"Light — light!" Faint as a sigh the response came, in the last motion of dying lips.

The night and the morning had met, day breaking in beauty on a human soul. In the evening time there was light.

IV.

"HE GIVETH HIS BELOVED SLEEP."

IF she could only get sleep, sound refreshing sleep. What would I not give for power to confer this blessing on my child! You must give her anodynes."

The doctor shook his head.

"Nature is taking care of this," he answered. "There come many periods of unconsciousness in every twenty-four hours. She has little snatches of slumber, by which the nerves are tranquilized and the body refreshed; and these are better for her than the heavy sleep of opium. Believe me that I am not indifferent to the case. No — no — my heart is in it. Were she my own child, she could hardly dwell more in my thoughts, nor tax in any higher degree my skill."

The doctor went away, and the mother returned to her place by the bedside of her sick child.

Care never failed — hand never wearied. Still love was bound in service. It could reach so far, and no farther. At the utmost limit of use it stood in tears over its own weakness, sighing "What would I not give to my beloved!"

"It is so hard to see her suffer; to know that she has not one hour of rest from pain — one night of peaceful sleep," said the mother to a friend, and the friend answered:

"It cannot last long. Soon there must come a sleep that will medicine all pain."

"You will kill me if you talk so!" A pang went through the mother's heart. "I cannot give up my precious child. I cannot — I will not see her die!"

A low cry of suffering came from the next room where the sick girl lay, and in a moment afterwards mother and friend were at the bedside.

"Where is the pain darling?" was the mother's anxious question.

A hand moved feebly, as if to touch the region of pain.

"Is it in your side?"

"Yes."

"Let me raise you higher on the pillow. There. Do you feel better now?"

But the forehead was not smooth, nor the mouth

placid. This change had wrought no ease, as the mother saw.

As they sat, bending towards her, the mother clasped her hands, and in half-despairing tones, said:

"Lord, give her sleep!"

There was a pause — a kind of hush — the penetration of a new sphere. Gradually, the countenance of the sick girl changed. The lines and indentations of her forehead, that it hurt you to look upon, smoothed themselves out; the lips softened; the lashes drooped, and lay without quivering, on her cheeks. How still the chamber grew!

"She is going to sleep," said the mother, whispering at the ear of her friend. "Do you think God heard me just now, and sent the rest and peace I asked for?"

"He is good — nay, goodness itself. His love for Mary is tenderer than even your love."

They drew back from the sleeper, noiselesssly, dropping the window curtains, that darkness might rest on her eyelids and weigh them down more surely.

"It can hardly be tenderer than mine. But, do you think God heard my prayer?" said the mother.

"You have prayed, many times that she might have sleep?"

"O yes."

"But never perhaps, in the same spirit that moved you just now. You felt helpless and despairing."

"Yes."

"Willing to abandon all, so that your precious one might be at peace. You cried out — 'Lord, give her sleep!' And, in that moment, you loosened your clasping arms. He has sent her sleep — if not in answer to your prayer, in answer, it may be, to your state — broken, at last, by suffering, into submission."

"Into submission!" There was a thrill of fear and pain in the mother's voice. "Submission to what?"

"His ways are not as our ways, dear friend! But they are always in mercy and loving kindness. And they will be so now. Could he have sent a greater blessing to this dear one than the sleep which now rests upon her like heaven's benediction!"

The mother did not answer, but sat in statue-like stillness, for a minute. Then rising, she drew back the window-curtain to let in the light again. Her manner was deliberate, yet under repression, as if she were holding down some struggling impulse. From the window she crossed to the bed, her friend, who had risen with her, moving at her side. Both stood, for a short space, looking down at the sleeper. Her countenance was even more placid than when they gazed upon it a little while before — softer and more infantile in its expression of repose.

"She sleeps sweetly," said the friend, in a whisper.

" Dear child ! " was breathed in response.

" What would *we* give to our beloved ? " resumed the friend,—" Wealth, and beauty, and all delight. But *He* giveth his beloved sleep. Your prayer is answered."

A wild paroxysm, and then a calmer state. Angels of consolation were present with the angels of resurrection; and while the latter were opening the gates of life, the former were giving peace.

" You would not awaken her from this sleep," said the friend, as they stood looking down afterwards upon the pure white vesture of clay, which the soul had put off for a body made of spiritual substance — imperishable and immortal; — stood looking down at the pure white vesture, lying in the perfume of bursting flowers, thrown over it by loving hands.

" He giveth his beloved sleep." This was the mother's answer, as she looked through tears, into the face of her friend. The angels of Consolation had not been with her in vain.

V.

IT IS WELL WITH THEM.

SHE lifted her sad, patient eyes to the speaker's face, and gazed at her steadily.

"When we say death, the angels understand resurrection."

Still no remark, but an earnest, questioning look.

"There is no death, in the sense you and I have understood the word. Does the worm really die, or only rise, through a wonderful transformation, into a higher state of being? Is it death, or only resurrection into a new life? And has the soul of man feebler vitality than the life-spark of a stupid grub? when its earthly state is completed, shall it not rise in a new and more beautiful body, made of spiritual substances, and with a new development of powers, infinitely transcending all mortal endowments?"

And still, there was no answer: but a few rays of light came into the sad eyes.

"Paul tells us that the invisible things of the other world may be understood by the things that appear in this. Let us take the birth of a lovely aeriel being simultaneously with the apparent death of a repulsive worm, as a type of the soul's resurrection. The worm did not really die, but its life put on in a new birth, higher beauty of form, and developed higher instincts. Before it was all of the earth, earthy; in its transformation, it became changed into a creature of more etherial substance, fitted to enjoy the heaven of sunshine, air, and flowers. If it is so with the worm in its death, what may we not hope and believe for man?"

"Oh, my sister," said the sad-eyed listener, speaking for the first time, and in a voice that was mournful as the sound of falling tears: "if I could but comprehend this — if I could only see anything but the grave's impenetrable darkness, and my babes lying there dead, I would feel like a new being. But I saw all beauty, sweetness, and love go out of their dear faces, and their soft flesh put on marble coldness. They were dead — dead! I thought my breath would stop when the close coffin lids shut over them: and I have felt the weight of earth that covers them, lying ever since their burial upon my heart. Dead — dead! The breath went out of them, and they were gone — gone forever!"

"It was a resurrection, dear Agnes!" replied the sister, who had come in her love, from a distant home, to speak words of consolation in a time of sorrow,—"A resurrection of their souls, clothed in forms of immortal beauty. When they ceased to breathe in this natural world, their lungs expanded with the air of a spiritual world, and their hearts, bounding with love, sent the currents of a heavenly vitality through all their veins. Look past the grave: past the shadows and darkness: past the cold dead clay. Your children are yet alive. What you saw buried, was only their cast-off earthly garments. They have garments now of spiritual substance, that cannot be soiled by evil, nor marred by sickness."

"If I could only be sure of this, sister," answered the bereaved one.

"From whence came the tender love that filled your heart, sister? Was it born of yourself? No. God gave it when he gave you those children. He sent this love for them into the world for their protection. It was his love, not yours; only yours as the children were yours. Can you believe this?"

The mourner was silent.

"From whence have you life?"

"It is God's gift."

"Yes. We have no life in ourselves; else would we be gods. If, therefore, life is God's gift, so are all good affections; and as a consequence that tenderest of all affections, a mother's love for her children. Now if mother-love is from God, will it not go with the children he takes from earth to heaven? And will he not give them into the care of angels? I can believe nothing else."

"It is a beautiful thought," said the sister, her sad eyes growing more luminous. "Oh, if it were to me an unquestioned truth!"

"Let your mind dwell upon it. Picture to yourself angelic homes, filled with the beauty, and grace, and happiness of childhood. Homes, into which there is the birth of a child simultaneously with the death of a child on earth. Think of your babes in one of those homes, lying on the breast of an angel, into whose heart God has given a fulness of mother-love as far above yours as are her celestial capacities."

Was that a smile winning its way over the face of sorrow? It was something so far removed from pain or grief, that it looked like a smile.

"If I were only certain that it was so with them!" she said, with an almost fluttering eagerness.

"Is it not a more rational thought than yours? More

rational than to think of so much beauty and sweetness, buried up in the earth? It was the loveliness of their souls that gave such exquisite grace to their bodies; their innocence that ensphered them with love, and made every motion, look, and tone so full of all winning attractions. This did not, and could not die. It was not flesh, but spirit. The soul merely laid off its robes of clay, to put on garments such as the angels wear."

"And you fully believe this, my sister?"

"As undoubtingly as I believe in my existence. Did not the Lord say of little children, ' Their angels do always behold the face of my father?' Take this as you will, and is it not an assurance to us, that children are under the especial care of angels? Not their bodies only, but in a more intimate degree, their immortal spirits, which are of infinitely more value than their bodies. Can this care and love cease when the clayey vesture is laid off forever?" No! For then, these loving angels —'their angels'— can have them more entirely as their own, and draw nearer to them, because all earthly and perverting influences are removed from their souls."

"Dear children!" said the sister, clasping her hands together, and looking upward with eyes full of light. "Dear, dear children! May it indeed be thus with you!

May you be in your Father's house, cared for by His angels."

"Doubt not for an instant," was replied to this — "not for a single instant! It is well with them; better even than your imagination, made fruitful by love, could portray. Does not the word Heaven include, in one thought, all perfection, all beauty, all felicity? Your babes are in Heaven. What more could you desire for them?"

"In Heaven; in Heaven!" The sister closed her eyes, and sat very still, trying to bridge the dark gulf of death, and walk over it in thought. She made the passage, and saw her babes on the other side. The grieving arch of her lips lost its clear outline in a smile that covered it like opening flowers.

"Yes, in Heaven, Agnes, where our mother went years ago."

"Dear mother! If she should know them as mine! Do you think that possible, sister?"

"Why not?"

"Oh, if I could believe that!" said the mourner.

"You may believe, dear sister, that God will let our mother know your babes, if in that knowledge would come to her any increase of happiness."

"Oh, I am sure it would make her happier," was answered, with a new-born enthusiasm. "How the thought warms my heart! Oh, sister! I feel that it must be as you say. That my lost ones are in a heavenly home."

"It is just as true, love, as that you and I are in an earthly home. There are two worlds; this natural world, and the spiritual world. Here, all forms are of natural substance — there, all forms are of spiritual substance. That world is the world of causes; this world the world of effects; and as all effects correspond with their causes, we may, with the clearest reason infer, that such things as exist here in a natural manner, exist in that world in a spiritual manner. If there are trees and flowers here — green fields and shining rivers — habitations — cities — garments — and the like, made of natural substances; is it any stretch of probability to conclude that all such things exist in the other world, but made of spiritual substances? Can we form any idea of a world without them? I cannot. We have permitted all ideas of the spiritual world to float through our minds in shapes indefinite, and this because in the word spirit we thought of something unsubstantial, like a breath of wind. But, really, our spirits are the only things substantial that we possess. Our bodies are frail, changing, and finite. In a few years they will cease to exist, and be absorbed wholly into elemental nature; but our souls are imperishable and eternal. And must not the world in which they are to live forever, be real and substantial? It is harder to doubt than to believe this. Agnes, my sister — there is a bridge of light across the river of death. Pass over it, in your thought, and stand securely on the other side. There are your babes; and let an assurance that it is well with them drive all the shadows from your soul, that peace may come in with sunshine."

And peace did come into the heart of the sorrowing one. Not in vain had been the sister's words of consolation. They covered up, as it were, from the mourner's eyes, the graves of her children, and showed her their forms, clothed in garments of such beauty as mortal eyes had never seen. They were no longer dead, but alive. The marble effigies, livid with signs of dissolution, and ghastly to behold, which she had lately remembered as all of her babes that love could cling to, faded from vision, — and in heavenly homes, with love, and life, and all of beauty around them, she saw the darlings of her soul.

It was well with them, and she believed it.

VI.

IF I HAD KNOWN OF THIS.

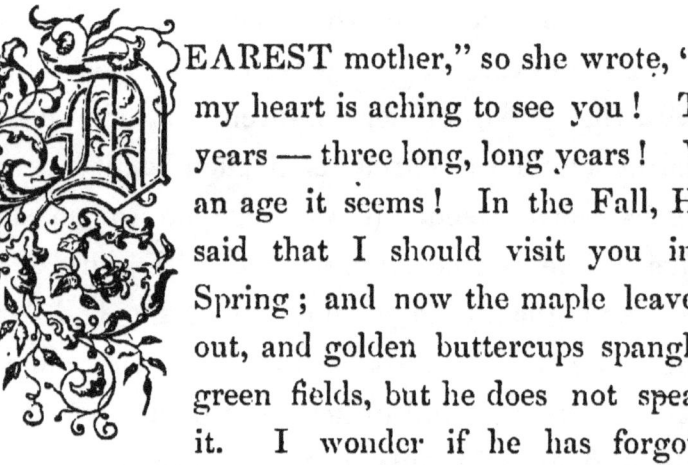"EAREST mother," so she wrote, "how my heart is aching to see you! Three years — three long, long years! What an age it seems! In the Fall, Henry said that I should visit you in the Spring; and now the maple leaves are out, and golden buttercups spangle the green fields, but he does not speak of it. I wonder if he has forgotten? How could he forget? Last evening I had it on my tongue to say that Spring was here, and did begin the sentence, but he interrupted me with a complaint about something wrong in our housekeeping matters, and I had no heart to touch the subject again. If things go wrong, and worry him, while I am here and trying to do my best, they would become intolerable during my absence. It is plain that I am not to see my dear old

home this Spring. Henry cannot spare me. Well, well; no doubt all is for the best. But, I am a weak child instead of a strong woman; a weak child, longing for my mother.

"Henry is kind — I love him, dear mother! Yes, I love my husband, oh so tenderly and so truly! I try to be a good wife; I try to enter into all his plans; to help him in everything. But, his heart is set on this world more than mine. He lives only for what is external, while my thought is all the while receding — all the while dwelling among things unseen. I am not as strong as I was last Spring, nor so stout. I looked over some of my dresses, laid by a year ago, and find that they will have to be taken in before I can wear them. I was surprised at this, for I haven't been sick — only a little drooping. My appetite was poor all winter, and is no better now. I try to eat, in order to keep up my strength, but have to force nearly every mouthful.

"Don't mind the stains on this page, mother; I can't keep my tears back while I write for thinking how only my poor written words will go to you — how, only, from this sheet I can look up into your dear, dear face, and not feast my living eyes upon you, nor clasp your neck, nor feel your kisses on my lips. Three years — such long years! Mother! oh, mother! what ails me?"

The pen dropped from nerveless fingers, and the writer's pale, gentle face, wet with tears, was laid upon the blotted sheet before her. Down stairs, in the room just beneath, sat Henry Willis, her husband, with busy brain. He was a strong, earnest man, whose heart was in his work. For three or four years he had been all absorbed in laying the foundation on which to build a temple dedicated to fortune; and now, the walls beginning to rise, he could think of little beyond the plans and progress of this temple. It was not designed to be very imposing or spacious, for his ideal was not grand; but such as it was, it had even while yet only shadowed forth, became the dwelling place of almost every thought.

Henry Willis had not forgotten his promise to let his wife visit her mother. All through the winter it had been remembered, if not spoken of, but with diminishing pleasure as the Spring approached. Now, he did not see that he could possibly let her go. Such absence would abridge his comfort materially; and beside, the expense troubled him. To fit her out with proper clothing for the visit, and pay the cost of travel, would not take less than one hundred dollars; and there were so many things he could do with this sum of money.

"I wonder she can think of going, when she knows what it will cost." So he was talking to himself in the room below, while she sat writing, as we have seen, above. "I work too hard for my money to throw it away after this fashion. I wish she took more interest in things; was as earnest to get ahead as I am. I don't understand her. It's as my father said before me — 'Women are riddles.' O, well! I must only make the best of it. Esther never crosses me in anything, and if I scold, never says a hard word back. I sometimes wish that she was sharper than she is, even if she was sharp on me sometimes. As to going home this Spring, I don't see that it is possible. There is too much to do, and I can't spare the money. She's said nothing about it, and I guess don't intend to. Maybe she's waiting for me to speak; or, maybe, she sees just how it is, and has concluded in her mind that it won't pay. Of course I shall make no allusion to the subject, if she doesn't. I don't understand this way some people have of looking back, and hankering after old places and former things. I look straight ahead, and build my hopes in the future. The past has little in it that I love or care for while the future is full of becoming pleasures. Ah, well! We're not all formed alike. It takes every kind to make a world."

How little did Henry Willis comprehend the woman he had taken to be his wife. Her gentleness, her sweetness, her tenderness had won him; but he was too much in the world, and a man of the world, to comprehend the wants of such a nature. His inner life reflected only external things — it was dark on the internal side.

There followed a kind of interregnum in the thought of Mr. Willis — a brief confusion — as he ceased speaking. Then he found himself listening, with pauses of the breath — listening upwards. He knew that his wife was in the room above. How very still it was! He could not hear a sound — not a footfall, or a movement of any kind. A weight of concern dropped suddenly on his feelings. Rising, he went up stairs, oppressed with a vague uneasiness.

"Esther!" he called, on opening the door of his wife's room, and seeing her at a small writing table, with her face bowed down and hidden. She did not stir nor answer. "Esther!" There was alarm in his voice now, as he crossed the floor quickly. "Esther!" he repeated, as he laid his hand on her. But there came no response. He tried to raise her head, but it sunk down from his imperfect hold; not, however, before he had seen her face, that was pale and death-like. His heart gave a wild bound of fear as he caught her in his arms, and carried her to the bed.

It was only a fainting fit; yet, not until long after the physician's arrival, did the weary soul take up its burden of mortal life again, and then only with a feeble effort.

To the husband's anxious inquiry — "What does it mean, doctor?" this, at first scarcely comprehended, answer was given: "There is some unsuppled want in her life, Mr. Willis. I have seen it for a long time. There are natnres which cannot live on bread alone, and her's, I think, is one of them. If you can discover and supply this want, well; if not, she will go on drooping and failing. A little while, and the grass will be green above her."

The physician understood, in part, the case, and this was his prescription — better than lancet or drug, than pill or powder.

Alone with his half unconscious wife, and the doctor's at first not clearly understood warning in his mind, Mr. Willis passed the night that followed — sleepless. He was wiser before the day dawned, for every word of that unfinished letter, over which the poor wife's heart and strength gave way, had been written down in his brain. It was read, and then the blotted pages laid carefully out of sight. But what a revelation it proved!

"If I had known of this!" How many times, in the long, sleepless hours of that night did Henry Willis thus give voice to his concern,— and all the while light came stealing into his mind with the gradual increase of breaking day. "Natures that cannot live on bread alone." Strange words when spoken by the doctor; but now full of meaning.

Back into the heart of this man, who had, for a few years, lost himself amid the attraction of mere sensuous things, came old ideals of life — old tendernesses — old appreciations — old loves.

"I have been too hard, and coarse, and cold, for this purer nature," he said, with brimming eyes, as he bent over the low breathing sleeper, and looked at her almost spiritual face. "And now, if I would keep her, I must be soft, and gentle, and warm. Drifting, drifting, drifting away, and I saw it not! The angel of my home, with wings half raised to depart, and I dwelling in conscious safety!"

He shuddered as he realized the danger that impended.

The day had broken, and now the morning sunbeams were looking in through the half-drawn curtains that shaded the windows of Mrs. Willis's bed-room. Mr. Willis, worn out with the night's watching, had laid his head upon a pillow, and was asleep. In the long rest of exhausted nature the wife had gathered up a portion of strength, and when the sunbeams awoke her, she looked around in bewilderment of mind. Partly rising on one arm, she saw her husband's face close beside her, on the very pillow which had supported her own head. He sat in a chair, with his clothes on, and was asleep.

"Henry!" She called his name, putting her hand on him as she spoke. Her voice and touch aroused the sleeper.

"How are you, darling?" He was wide awake in a moment, looking at her with tender, yet troubled eyes.

"I'm very well. What has been the matter, Henry? Why are you sitting here with your clothes on? Have I been sick?" Mrs. Willis, with whom memory was becoming active, looked from her husband's face to the table where she had been writing.

"You had a fainting spell, dear," was answered, and as Mr. Willis said this, he pressed his wife gently back upon the pillow from which she had arisen. "I never dreamed you were getting so weak. But I see it all now. We strong, rough men, don't comprehend everything."

A soft smile went faintly over the pale face of Mrs. Willis, giving it a sad and touching beauty. Her silken lashes fell trembling down on her cheeks. Her wan lips quivered. Now the doctor's admonition came in full force to her husband, and all it meant was apprehended. He felt that to lose her, would be to lose that which made life really precious. The old true love, that had in it no worldliness — that was so full of sweetness — that saw its object as an embodiment of purity and grace — was revived in his heart, and he wondered how it could ever have failed.

"As soon as you are strong enough, Esther, to bear the journey, you must make that visit to your mother. If I had known — " The husband checked himself, for this was betraying the fact that he had read her un- unfinished letter.

"I am strong enough, Henry." Her eyes flashed open, and he saw rainbows in the tears that gemmed her lashes.

"You want to see your mother very much?"

"Oh, Henry!" The wet lids quivered and closed. "Three years is a long, long time, Henry," she murmured, with her eyes still closed.

"I know it is darling. But I was so absorbed in my work — so lost in business and plans — that I did not enter as I should have done, into your feelings. But I see it all now. You shall go home at once, and every year, if your heart desires it.

What light, and warmth, and beauty, came into the pale, wasted countenance!

"You are very good, Henry; and it will be selfish in me to leave you, even for a short time; but I am not so strong as I was, dear. Somehow, I am giving way both outwardly and inwardly. For the whole of last year, I have pined to see my old home — to lay my head against my mother, and to feel her arms around me. I could not help it, dear, though I tried hard. You are good and kind; I love you with my whole heart; and I ought not to feel as I have felt."

The eyes of Mrs. Willis were full of love as she looked up into her husband's face.

"If I had only known of this! And I might have known," was the self-condemning answer.

In less than a week Mrs. Willis was in her mother's arms. Her husband stood by, comprehending in a slight degree, through recently obtained perceptions, something of her ineffable joy. She was passing away from him, but he had drawn her back.

Thenceforth, food, other than natural bread, was given for the sustenance of a life whose wants reached far above the things that perish in the using.

VII.

HE CAME IN MERCY

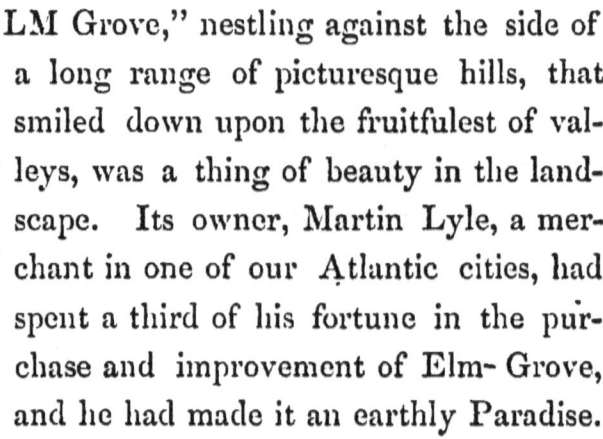"ELM Grove," nestling against the side of a long range of picturesque hills, that smiled down upon the fruitfulest of valleys, was a thing of beauty in the landscape. Its owner, Martin Lyle, a merchant in one of our Atlantic cities, had spent a third of his fortune in the purchase and improvement of Elm-Grove, and he had made it an earthly Paradise. Taste, pride, and love of nature had, in turn, stimulated his thoughts and moved his hand in the work of adornment, until beauty covered all things like a garment. Business became a secondary interest in his mind; love of gain burned feebly; trade was irksome; the city an offence. And so Martin Lyle withdrew from active business life, and retired with his family to Elm Grove.

But from the day of this change in the order of his

life, a dimly obscuring veil seemed to fall on every thing around him. Elm Grove lost beauty in his eyes. Mr. Lyle moved through his gardens and groves, his lawns and summer-houses, and tried to force enjoyment; but in this very effort interest failed. He was resting for happiness in the excellence of outward, instead of inward life; and having touched the outward at nearly all desirable points, weariness was beginning to weigh upon his spirit.

Mr. Lyle was one of that large class of persons who live only for themselves and families. Outside of his own little world, he had few interests. He was a useful man so long as he engaged actively in business; for then, in the ardor of self-service, he became the servant of good to others through the common benefits that flow from trade. But when he retired from business, with the end of simply enjoying himself, he became a drone in society. An idler, for the most part, suffering the idler's penalty of weariness and unrest.

As Mr. Lyle regarded life, so it was regarded by his family. They did not consider themselves as members of the common body in the degree involving mutual service. To receive and to enjoy included their whole philosophy. The use of such talents and skill as they possessed in the work of good to others, was a thought which had never come into their minds. Wealth had given them superiority and immunity; so believing and so acting, the possession of wealth was hurtful — hurtful to their souls, and therefore destructive of happiness.

Daily, through all the luxuriant summer, from hundreds of lips fell the words, " How beautiful ! " And in hundreds of hearts a pulse of envy beat, as eyes dwelt in admiration on Elm Grove and its magnificent surroundings. But with each rising and falling day of that fruitful summer, hearts grew more and more shadowed in Elm Grove. It had not fulfilled the enticing promise that lured its owner away from the city and its bustling marts.

But separated as Mr. Lyle was from business, no thought of going back found place for a moment. Relieved from that perpetual tension of mind which always accompanies trade, he experienced a kind of negative enjoyment in his comparative idleness, not to be willingly exchanged for the old state.

Before removing permanently to his elegant country home, Mr. Lyle had, during several years of carefully planned culture, made everything so perfect that little remained to be accomplished. Fruition was now to come. But it was inadequate — strangely in defect of anticipation. He had little to do, for all was done; and it is in doing that we find real pleasure, not in the contemplation of what is done.

One day, after the fields had given their harvests to the reapers; after the trees had bestowed their fruit, and the vines their clusters, in the late, still autumn time, when the heart grows pensive or sad, as we look on decaying nature, Mr. Lyle sat dreamily gazing forth upon the landscape. He was alone, and had been alone for some time. There was a deeper shadow than usual on his feelings; we say deeper, meaning to convey the impression that he rested now under a shadow all the while. A step approached, but he did not seem to observe the presence of any one. A hand was laid upon his shoulder. He turned, slightly starting, and said:

"Oh, it's you, Harriet?"

"You are sober, dear. What are you thinking about?" Mrs. Lyle sat down by her husband, and looked at him earnestly.

"I feel sober," was the reply.

"What is there to shadow your feelings?"

Mr. Lyle shook his head, and murmured, in a half absent way: "Nothing."

"What have you been thinking about?" Mrs. Lyle repeating her first question.

"About many things that I do not see clearly," he answered. "I'm afraid, Harriet, that I have not understood life. What more have I desired than this?" and he swept his hand and eyes around the meadows and woodlands that lay within the compass of Elm Grove. "And yet, since I have tried to enjoy it fully, I seem not to have enjoyed it at all."

There was in the tone and expression of her husband something that made a low fear creep through the heart of Mrs. Lyle. She knew that he had not been happy since his withdrawal from business, and idle life at Elm Grove; but no utterance like this had before given voice to a disquiet spirit. What answer could she make? None came to her lips, and so she sat in silence, gazing upon his shadowed face, and into his strangely altered eyes.

"I put my heart in this." And again he swept his hand towards the scenery that surrounded them. "I planned for years our paradise, into which no evil thing was to intrude. I was to sit down among its beauties, no man being my peer in happiness. But there was an error somewhere in my calculation. It has not come out as I expected. Ah, me! I do not understand myself!" And laying his head down in his hands, he clasped his temples and sighed heavily.

Ah, how many there are who, like our retired merchant, find life a mystery — how many who, like him, in summing up the result towards which they have been looking with hopeful anticipations, find that there has been an error in the calculation!

Mrs. Lyle sat down beside her husband, strangely questioning in her mind as to the state into which he had fallen, and unable to meet it by a single rightly spoken word. She drew her hands within one of his arms, and leaned her face against him. A great shadow fell upon her; a low shudder of fear, as though an invisible danger were approaching, crept through her heart.

"What more could I have asked?" Mr. Lyle gave voice to his thoughts again. "I have made of Elm Grove all that I designed — all that fancy pictured. It is perfect; and yet, day by day enjoyment wanes."

But his wife had no medicine for his sick soul. Like him, she had lived only in the outer world; had built only on the foundations of natural life.

From that period Mr. Lyle fell into a listless, dreamy state. For hours every day he would sit alone; and if intruded upon, show signs of impatience. All interest in Elm Grove departed; yet he resisted every effort of his wife and daughters to gain his consent to a removal. The winter that followed was one of new and painful experiences to the family. Trouble came in too appalling shapes. In withdrawing from business, Mr. Lyle had left four-fifths of his capital in the firm, besides retaining an interest. Through bad debts and failing speculations, it happened that the entire capital was lost.

The balance sheet and account of stock taken in January, revealed a startling fact. The house was bankrupt! The announcement of this disaster, coming as it did upon a morbid and depressed condition of mind, swept away the already wavering reason, and Mr. Lyle floated helplessly down the stream of life.

It is difficult to imagine a deeper despair than that into which Mrs. Lyle and her two daughters were suddenly plunged. They had not been educated, in any thing, for a trial like this. In the darkness that surrounded them, no path was visible; no light appeared. For a little while they sat down with folded hands, helpless and hopeless.

But love is a vital thing; and love soon stirred the thought of Mrs. Lyle. One suggestion after another came; and, as her soul sat listening in the silence and darkness in which it dwelt, she heard voices never heard before, and a speech full of new and inspiring utterances. She had likewise, faint glimpses of an inner world, and of ends and deeds in life based on higher principles. Love made living a sense of duty. In her hour of extremest weakness, strength was born — born of God's spirit as it moved over the face of the great deep in her soul.

The form of Mr. Lyle's insanity was an impassive, almost lifeless condition of mind. There were no lurid gleams of blind passion, or exhibition of a strong will in a wrong direction. He was harmless, and yielding almost implictly to his wife. He was not, therefore, removed to an asylum.

The wreck of misfortune was complete. Elm Grove passed into other hands, and the family came back to the city; but how different their position from that occupied a little while before. Then only the question of how to enjoy life occupied their thoughts; now it was the question of sustaining life.

Where an earnest purpose to do exists, ways and means usually appear, though not always in the direction anticipated. Not only did light come to the mother in darkness, but to her two daughters, Grace and Harriet, also. They had minds and hands; and as by these others did useful service in the world, through which sustenance of life came, might not they do useful service also? The question was not long in gaining an affirmative answer. Their father's helplessness, and their mother's years, were an ever present motive. Love moved them to action, and ere a twelvemonth passed from the time they went forth shuddering into the world from their Eden at Elm Grove, they were bringing in full sheaves from their fields of labor, and laying them, in tears of hope and thankfulness, on the threshing floor of home.

A new sphere of life was gradually developed from a new order of life in the stricken, but closer bound family. The light which had shone in upon them, when all was dark, and the voices with new utterances which had come to them in the silence of their despair, continued to shine with increasing brightness, and to speak in a more emphatic language. They saw into a new world of thought and motive, and understood life from higher principles. Existence had gained a new signification.

How tenderly, how devotedly, how yearningly did they minister to that beloved one, who had been stricken in the prime of manhood. All they had lost of worldly good and worldly possession, was as nothing to their loss of his clear reason and loving consciousness; and with the care and tenderness of a mother seeking to touch the springs of thought in her infant, did they seek to awaken in his mind the orderly activities of a conscious soul. And their loving care did not lie fruitless. Oh, with what thrills of genuine pleasure did they hail the first signs of returning reason! How toil grew light, and self-denial easy, as they saw scale after scale drop away from his eyes, and his vision grow clearer and clearer.

There was a new element in the life of this family upon which rested their higher development. Misfortune is a wise teacher; but unless God is acknowledged in misfortune, and the soul accepts the wisdom that comes from God, the teaching but little avails. It availed here, because the new element of religious trust found an abiding place with Mrs. Lyle, and passed by spiritual transfusion to the hearts of her daughters. There had been loss and gain; but, in adjusting the account, how largely proved the gain.

One day, it was nearly two years from the time when darkness fell upon them so suddenly, Mrs. Lyle entered a room where Grace, her oldest daughter, sat alone. She held a note in her hand, and also a newspaper. Grace looked up with a quiet smile on her womanly face.

"This is from Henry Lardner," said Mrs. Lyle, holding out the note.

Instantly a warm flush mantled the daughter's brow.

"He is worthy, my child, and I cannot answer nay." Mrs. Lyle bent down and kissed her, and then received the hidden face on her bosom.

"A sad thing has happened," said Mrs. Lyle, a little while afterward. "A very sad thing."

"What?" A shadow fell over the glowing countenance of Grace.

Mrs. Lyle opened the newspaper in her hand and read:

"Theodore Flemming was arrested at his home last evening, charged with participation in a system of gigantic frauds against the customs revenue. The proofs of his complicity are ample. He has only been married a few months to the daughter of a prominent citizen. The circumstance has deeply shocked our community."

Mrs. Lyle looked up as she finished reading. The countenance of Grace was deadly pale.

"My daughter!" she said, dropping the paper and drawing an arm around Grace; "Theodore Flemming is nothing to you!"

"Nothing, mother," was calmly answered. "Nothing now. When misfortune fell upon my life, he turned away coldly, and made his promise false. Oh, thank God for misfortune!"

"Yes, thank God, my child! His ways are in the dark; they are past finding out; but His steps are sure. He comes to us ever in mercy, leading us by ways that we know not."

The door opened, and the placid face of a man looked in. It was the face of Mr. Lyle, in which the light of reason shone — not with the strong light as of old, but steady and full of promise.

"Have you heard the news about Flemming?" he asked.

"I was just reading it to Grace," replied Mrs. Lyle.

For a few moments he looked curiously and half in doubt at Grace. Then crossing the room, and laying his hand upon her head, uttered these words:

"We shall see it all clear enough by and by, darling. God is good, and will make it plain. It seems to be coming out right, as mother said it would come," glancing with a look of loving confidence towards his wife. "I thought it would have killed me, when the blow came. Ah well, dear! Never mind. There's something good in store for us."

And there was, in a truer, higher, and more heavenly life, into which, by daily duties, they entered more and more. They had gone down, as into the valley and shadow of death; and now, rising on the other side, were already ascending the mountains, in whose far-reaching summits angels have their dwelling places. Yes, God in his providence had come to them in mercy; and while removing the foundations on which their house was builded, and letting the fair structure fall into hopeless ruin, was spreading beneath them His everlasting arms. He cast down that he might raise them up again; He wounded to heal; shadowed their natural lives, that he might open to them the windows of Heaven, and flood their souls with the marvelous radiance of the upper world.

Wealth never came back to them, nor did the mind

of Mr. Lyle gather up its full strength again. But sweet peace dwelt with them, as in patience and loving self-devotion they builded new dwelling-places for the soul, against which earthly storms might beat in vain, for they were founded on a rock.

VIII.

ONE DAY AT A TIME.

ONE neighbor dropped in upon another.

"Are you sick, Mrs. Carson?" asked the visitor, on meeting a pale, troubled face.

"Sick at heart, Mary," was answered, gloomily. Not even the ghost of a smile became visible.

"Is that all?" The visitor's countenance brightened.

Mrs. Carson looked half surprised and half offended.

"I don't know any worse sickness," she said, rather fretfully.

"That depends on the origin and nature of the disease," replied the friend. "There is a heart-sickness, which is unto death; but I take it that yours is of a milder type, having its origin among life's petty annoyances, or it may be in its more sober disappointments; in things common to us all, yet borne in so many different ways."

Mrs. Carson sighed heavily. There was a leaden weight on her bosom. Reason assented to her visitor's suggestions, but oppressed feeling held her in painful bondage.

"What troubles you to-day? Why are you so much cast down?" asked the visitor. "But this may be an intrusion."

Mrs. Carson did not answer immediately. Her dreary eyes rested on the floor; her hands lay idly in her lap; she was the picture of despondency. At length, she said:

"Owing to changes in business, my husband must give up his situation. A dissolution in the firm throws him out. To-morrow he leaves his place, with no prospect of another. What are we to do? We've saved nothing. How could we, on so light an income."

"I'm sorry to hear that," answered the lady. "Very sorry."

"Could anything be more gloomy or discouraging? Can you wonder that I am in trouble?"

"I do not wonder that you are concerned about the future, Mrs. Carson. That is a natural result. But I cannot see, in the event, any reason why you should sit down with folded hands, and make yourself miserable. Mr. Carson is, of course, troubled."

"You may well say that. He took scarcely a mouthful of breakfast this morning."

"On him rests the heaviest part of this burden. He must provide and maintain a home for his wife and children. I sympathize with him from my heart."

"It's seeing him so cast down that makes me so wretched," said Mrs. Carson. "If he were cheerful and hopeful, I could take heart."

"Perhaps, in thought, he is saying the same thing of you."

A flash of surprise came into Mrs. Carson's face. The suggestion of her friend went home.

"When did he tell you of this?"

"Last night. I saw that something was troubling him, and urged him to say what it was. Then he told me."

"How did you receive the announcement?"

Mrs. Carson was silent.

"Bravely, as a wife should, when she sees trouble approaching her husband, or in weakness and tears?"

"In weakness and tears. I make you this confession."

"Did that help him any? Did that make his trouble lighter?"

4

"No, no, my friend. While telling me of the change, he mingled hopeful words in his sentences. But afterwards he sat silent and gloomy through all the evening."

"And you?"

"Cried myself almost sick."

"And sat opposite to him, at breakfast time this morning, with a rueful visage. No wonder he had no appetite."

"No wonder," said Mrs. Carson, repeating the words to herself. "That was not well, at least."

"And should not be repeated."

"It shall not be repeated, Mary. Poor man! He has enough to bear, without the dead weight of my despondency."

"I'm glad to hear you say that, Mrs. Carson. Now you are coming towards the right way of thinking. We have only to-day, and in every to-day we shall find the elements of peace, if we will search for them; and the elements of disquietude as well. To accept the one, and reject the other, is to be wise. Last evening you cast aside your husband's hopeful words, and drew around both his heart and yours a pall of despondency. This morning your state was unchanged, and you let him go forth for the day doubly weighted. My friend, this was not well. Now, I pray you, limit thought and duty, as far as in you lies, to this one day which, in God's providence, is yours. You have a pleasant home, children, a husband. There is not a single external element, in all appertaining to your *to-day*, that is not favorable to peace of mind. When to-morrow becomes to-day, will the change be marked? I think not. You will still, I trust, have your home, food, raiment, your children and your husband, and God's promise to those who do their duty in singleness of heart. What if your husband's hands are idle for a short time? What if the way, looking weeks or months in advance, does not seem clear? Your to-day is all bright, if you will but have it so. The sun shines, the heart beats, God's providence is not hindered. You may be in peace, if you will do your best to secure peace."

The friend departed, leaving Mrs. Carson in a better frame of mind, and with her thoughts flowing in the right direction. "One day at a time. One day at a time," she said to herself, as her hands took hold upon the duties of the hour. "Ah! if we could so live, how tranquil all might be. Even in this feeble effort, my heart has a calmer beat. I did not believe in the possibility of a change such as I feel. One day at a time!"

She lingered on the suggestion, drawing out more and more distinctly many of the things it involved, and seeing more and more clearly, how it lay at the basis of all right living and true enjoyment.

Relieved, in a great measure, from its burden of despondency, the mind of Mrs. Carson lifted itself into a region of clearer light, and became busy with ways and means adapted to the change which had taken place in their circumstances. Instead of remaining with folded hands, in terror of approaching ills, or dwelling in vague apprehensions, she let hope gain entrance; and hope had good words to say.

Slowly, in the dimly closing twilight, a man walked, with eyes upon the pavement — walks with bowed head and stooping shoulders; he was bending under a heavy weight. One week ago, the same man walked in the twilight, with head erect, and quickly falling footsteps, almost impatient to reach his home. Then, he looked for a smiling welcome and loving words; now, as thought reached forward, he saw only clouds and tears. His heart was cheerful then, but heavy now. Suddenly, his path had been crossed by a mountain range that looked impassable. For himself, he might gird his loins, and bravely move to the ascent; but, she who must walk by his side through smiling landscapes, or amid toilsome acclivities, had sunk down, overcome by weak terrors; and with this added, how was he to advance? Brave enough to face the mountain, with its sky-reaching cliffs and snowy summits, if his way must be over its barrier, and strong enough to support his companion, if she put forth what strength was given, he was not able to carry her as a dead weight. And this it was that bowed his head and saddened his spirit, as he lingered, with slow steps, in the falling shadows, and dreaded the arrival at home.

Mr. Carson's hand rested for some moments on the door, before he found heart to push it open. Night had fallen without; but a darker night seemed waiting for him within — a night, the blackness of which no lamp rays could penetrate. Usually, he shut the door after him with a quick, strong hand, that announced his entrance in echoes from the farthest chambers, and made the stairs musical with the patter of little feet; now it was closed so noislessly, that only the alert ears of Mrs. Carson noted his coming.

"There's your father," she said to three little ones who had gathered about the centre table, under a gas lamp, one with her doll, and two with picture books, and then there was a scampering down stairs, and a jangling of young voices, sweet, if discordant. The mother heard only the sound of kisses in response. The father's voice, lately so full of glad welcomes, as he opened his arms for his babies, was silent now. What a change! And yet so far as every external element of happiness was concerned, no new condition existed. There was no evil in the present. Food and raiment, light and warmth, health — all that they could appropriate was in equal abundance now as before. It was the shadow of some imagined evil in the future, which might never come, that shut the sunlight from their hearts — which might never come, or, coming, change to good in the day of its advent.

Mr. Carson entered the room where his wife sat, bearing one child in his arms, while two clung to him, in laughing efforts to impede his progress. The old welcoming smile was on her face, not so bright nor so happy, but fuller of tenderness. How like a flash its reflected rays drank up the shadows from his eyes and brow. He could not help stooping over and kissing her with unwonted fervor. She felt it, in a sweet thrill, down to her heart. They were drawing closer together.

"You have changed since morning," said Mr. Carson, soon after, as the children resumed their toys and picture books, laying his hand on his wife's head as he spoke, and looking into her calm eyes almost wonderingly.

"Have I?"

"Yes. What has brought this change?"

"Right thinking, perhaps."

"What have been your thoughts?"

"To-day is ours, and only to-day.

"Only to-day," said Mr. Carson echoing the words of his wife.

"Is it wise to throw aside the good things of to-day, because in doubt as to the future? To shut our windows, and refuse to let to-day's sunshine enter our dwellings, because there are signs of a storm to-morrow?"

"No, it is not wise," answered the husband.

"So I have thought, and so thinking, I have been striving to keep myself in the present, and amid the duties and blessings that crowd the passing hours. All is well with us to-day — all has been well with us so far in life; and if changes and trials are to come, will not strength as we need be given?"

"Surely it will, dear wife!" said Mr. Carson. "I cannot express the feeling of relief your language gives. Yes, yes. Let us take, in all our to-days, the good things God has provided. Hitherto they have been in full measure. If diminished from this time, as to what is external and material, may we not have an increase of our internal pleasures? I do not think we have been a great deal happier since a better income enabled us to rent this larger house, and to possess costlier furniture."

"Just the conclusion of my own mind," answered the wife. "I know we were as happy — sometimes I have thought, happier — in that cosy little house where the first six years of our wedded lives were spent. And now that you have alluded to this humble condition, I will say what further has been in my thoughts. Let us go back to the same condition, and thus reduce our expenses to the old rate. In a smaller house, I can get along well enough with a single servant, and not have to work any harder than I do now. This will be acting right in the present — doing to-day what seemeth best — and I think we shall find the way before us growing smooth to our feet, though it look so rough and so thorny in prospective."

"Comforter! — consoler! — strengthener!" said Mr. Carson, giving way to a gush of feeling. His voice was half-choked and his eyes glistened. "One hour ago, I was wretched. Now I am hopeful, resigned, peaceful. The high mountain across my path, that seemed impassable, has sunk to a little hill. When our feet begin the ascent, we shall not find the way so very difficult; and strength will come in the hour of need."

And it came as he had prophesied. The lesson and the experience of that day and evening to Mr. and Mrs. Carson were so full of instruction, that they could not be forgotten. In present right thinking and acting — in taking each day as it came, and accepting the good it had to offer — they found tranquility of mind; but, in all variations from this rule of life — in all weak yieldings to doubt and fear — in all helpless broodings over coming ill — they were led into darkness, self-torments, wretchedness. One day at a time — taking and using the good it had to offer, and bearing patiently its ills — this was the better life they sought to live; and though, for some years afterwards, their way in the world was through obscure places, where the humbler move, they found as sweet flowers to give the air perfume, and as soft and green a turf for their feet, as had ever delighted them in more prosperous seasons.

IX.

THE ANGEL-SISTER.

"ALMOST a woman!" says Mrs. Wayland glancing after her daughter, who was leaving the room. And then she sighed; and her eyes looked dreamily inward; and she sat very still, like one asleep.

Almost a woman! Yes; Lucy's slender form had sprung up rapidly in the past year, and her limbs and bust had rounded into beautiful symmetry.

What was in the mother's thoughts that she sighed? Did she fear for the woman's life of her darling? Had her own experiences been so sad that she could not look with sunny hope into the future of her child? Not that. The sigh had another meaning. Always she saw, moving beside Lucy, another form, growing as she grew, and reaching with her toward the sweet ripeness of womanhood; and the sigh was for that form, because to all but herself it was invisible. Just five years before that form of a twin-sister vanished from her home and was seen not there again.

"If Mary had not died!" Ah, did she ever look at Lucy that these words came not to shadow her feelings? "If Mary had not died," followed like a spectre, the sentence: "Almost a woman!"

"What a loss to poor Lucy!" So ran her thoughts as she sat very still, like one asleep under the pressure of feeling. "Mary would have been every thing to her. Sister, companion, friend, counsellor, comforter. Now she must go forth in life alone. No sister to stand by her side and make her strength double in trial; for that she will have in full measure. It comes to all."

"How differently she would have developed," went on the mother, in her thoughts, "If Mary had not died! There was just enough of dissimilarity in their characters to give life, action, and harmony to both. Mary was quieter and graver; she would have matured faster; all the better for Lucy. Ah, it was a loss that must ever be felt as irreparable. Why do such things happen? It is of Providence, they say, and for the best. I can not see it." And Mrs. Wayland sighed heavily.

"Dear, angel Mary!" she went on. "How the

light faded when your life went out! How the music ceased when your voice grew silent! I can never see it to be right; never, never. Poor Lucy! I wonder sometimes that she can be so gay of heart. If she comprehended her loss as I comprehend it, she would hardly smile again. The time will come when her heart will cry out in its loneliness, pain, or sorrow,— 'Oh my sister! Why were you taken from me?'"

As she thus mused and murmured, the Angel of Sleep laid her soft touch on the mother's heavy eyelids, and her spirit went away into the land of dreams. It was with her now as of old. Side by side walked her twin children through the sunny chambers of her home, and their blending voices made music for her heart all the day long. Swiftly the years went by. Up from blossomy girlhood they passed to ripe young womanhood; and then came young wooers to win them away from her, and bear them off to other homes. Mary went first, and to a far distance. A thousand miles were stretched between them. Then Lucy laid her hand, lovingly and trustingly, into the hand of one who promised to make all her life rich with blessing. She did not, like Mary, go afar off, but kept near her old home.

The years came and went, bringing their burdens of care and their lessons of disappointment. Lucy had a large share of these, and under the burdens she bent wearily and often in pain.

"If Mary were only here! If I could listen to her voice! If I could lean my head upon her as of old!"

How often she said this sadly and tearfully. But Mary was far away sighing over her own depressing cares, or fainting amidst her trials. Nor, if distance had been removed, would the presence of Mary have given either strength or comfort, for she stood in need of both for herself. They might have wept together, and there would have been a sad pleasure in this; but in suffering both had grown selfish, and asked, but had nothing to give.

Then a deeper trouble came to Lucy. Death stole silently into her home at evening after the sun went down, and when the morning broke one whose life-pulses had taken their beat from her own was not. Bowing down her head, she refused to be comforted.

"Oh, if Mary were only here!" said the mother, as she went, almost in despair, from the chamber where Lucy sat in marble-like stillness. "If Mary were only here! Her voice would find its way to her heart; her words would come to her in consolation."

A letter was placed in her hands. It was from Mary. She opened it and read:

"Dear Mother,— Baby is dead, and my heart is broken! Will you not come to me?"

"Only a dream!" said a soft, low voice, musically.

The mother looked up and saw before her a woman, whose calm face and loving eyes made her think of the eyes and face of an angel. A deep peace fell upon her spirit.

"Only a dream of what might have been, if Mary were not in heaven!"

A thrill of pleasure ran through the heart of Mrs. Wayland, and she lifted her soul in thankfulness. "Baby is dead, and my heart is broken!" No, no. That piercing cry would never come from her lips.

And now the old life goes on, but with a change that, while it is wonderful, excites no feeling of wonder in the mind of Mrs. Wayland. In thought she had always seen the dead twin-sister moving beside the living twin-sister, like a shadowy phantom. Now she was near her like a living presence, full of life and tender love, yet visible to no mortal eyes but the mother's. Sleeping or waking, she was always near to Lucy, but nearest in sleep, and most watchful. Her influence over her was almost inperceptible, but certain as the influence of dew and sunshine upon the earth. Mrs. Wayland noted it from day to day in pious thankfulness.

"God has not separated them," she said, "but made of one a guardian angel to the other. How passion and selfishness, after darkening the fair horizon of her mind for a little season, pass away like threatening clouds under the influence of right thoughts and gentle affections, which glide into her mind and heart from the soul of her angel-sister! Dear Mary! Oh if I could take you into my arms! If I could hold you to my bosom, what infinite joy would be mine! When Lucy weeps, what loving sympathy softens all your heavenly countenance, and how closely you draw near her! When she is tempted, your lips approach her ears with words of strength and assurance. I see daily the wonder-working power of your presence over her. Not dead and absent! Oh no. But living and present; present in greater power, and for higher good, than is possible in any mortal nearness."

And so life went on from day to day, and from year to year, the angel-sister always intimately present, and visible only to the mother's eyes. Then Lucy went out from her home a bride, and in the years that followed came trials and sorrows such as had never shadowed her heart even dimly in imagination; such trials and sorrows as come to all in some degree. Yet never, in all these years, was Mary afar off, but always intimately near; with aid in trial, strength in weakness, and comfort when the heart was bowed down, and the eyes wet with tears. It was wonderful to see how, like the influence of some magic spell, the presence of Mary, unseen and unknown, would change the thoughts and feelings of Lucy, and bring her mind from darkness into light. Often at these times Lucy would lift her eyes upward, and murmur some words from the Book of books, the memory of which her angel-sister had uncovered.

Once, overcome with weariness, Lucy had fallen asleep with her baby in her arms. Mary was always most watchful over her, as we have said, in sleep. So now she drew closer, and her eyes did not wander a moment from the faces of the babe and its mother. Soon there came a shade of concern in the calm face of the angel-watcher, as if danger were approaching; but she did not look up nor around. Now, with a feeling of terror, Mrs. Wayland saw a hideous serpent come stealing in through the open door. She could not move nor cry out, but sat powerless, as in a frightful nightmare. Gradually it approached the unconscious sleepers, its head erect and its venomous eyes glaring in fiery eagerness. Then the guardian's lips bent down to the ears of Lucy and awakened her with a dream. She sprang up with a cry, clasping, as she did so, her baby to her bosom. The danger was past. She did not even know that there had been danger, for the serpent, the instant she moved, glanced from the room like lightning.

At another time Lucy was riding with her husband along a road that lay upon the brink of a precipice. The slightest forgetfulness or want of care in driving might prove fatal. Just as they were approaching a narrow point where the wheels must come within a few inches of the unguarded edge, Mrs. Wayland noticed a dark, shadowy form close to Lucy's husband, whispering in his ear, and gaining his attention. His hand, in forgetfulness, let the reins fall loose, and the carriage wavered from the arrowy line in which it had been moving. But the angel saw the fiend, who fled at a glance from her glittering eyes, and, on his guard again in an instant, the driver passed the dangerous place in safety.

"Thank God for such wonderful care!" said Mrs. Wayland, in her heart. Thus Lucy was protected through the mediation of her sister, as well as strengthened and comforted.

At last the trouble of all troubles for a mother's heart came. A little one, that had become as a part of her life, came down with its tender feet to the brink of Death's river. Was there no eye to pity, and no hand to save? Lucy was wild with fear and anguish, and in the bitterness of her suffering prayed for the life of her child. In all these hours of pain the angel-sister stood bending over her — now with a hand on her throbbing temples, now with her head drawn lovingly against her bosom, and now breathing into her ears precious truths for consolation. That all this was not in vain the mother saw; for calmer states would supervene, and periods of deep tranquillity follow upon wild excitement.

At last the shadowy curtain fell on the brief drama of that young child's life, and for a time Lucy refused to be comforted, shutting her ears to all the words of healing that friends, seen and unseen, could offer. She called God cruel for taking her babe.

The day which dawned on that night of sorrow, when the baby went up to heaven, passed heavily away, and still the stricken mother turned herself from all who tried to lift her thoughts toward the eternal mansions. Darkness fell upon nature again, and in the stillness that followed, Lucy slept. Mrs. Wayland, to whose eyes the form of Mary was always visible, now saw her weaving a dream for the inner eyes of the sleeper. It was to her as a representation. First appeared to the sorrowing mother a green bank, dotted over with flowers. Around the foot a pleasant stream twined its clear waters like a silver cord. Next appeared children on the bank with garlands of flowers, sporting with each other. They were the happiest children she had ever looked upon. As she gazed she heard music, and the words of singers:

"He leadeth them beside still waters."

"And this is heaven!" said the mother, in her dream.

"Yes," said a beautiful maiden, in shining white garments, coming to her side. "This is heaven; and these are the little ones whom the loving Father of us all has translated from a world of sorrow and pain to this world of blessedness."

"I have lost a child!" The sorrowing mother spoke eagerly. "A little while ago I looked my last on his dying face. Oh, is my child here? My precious child!"

"Come," said the maiden. The scene changed. They were in a beautiful apartment, the halls of which were of gold and all precious stones, that shone resplendently. Soft, silvery curtains, floating in the perfumed air, hung over and around a bed of downy softness. Sitting by this bed, and bending over it in an attitude of loving care, bent another maiden of wondrous beauty. The mother drew near. A babe was lying on the bed; her own lost darling; she knew him at a glance!

"You have come for him?" said the maiden, looking up into the mother's face.

"Yes," she answered. "I can not part with my baby. I must have him back again."

An expression of regret dimmed the angel brightness

of the maiden's countenance. But she bent over the child, and lifting him gently, laid her lips upon his forehead with a kiss of the tenderest love. Then placing him in the mother's arms, she said,

"Take him back to sorrow, to suffering, and to pain. But oh, guard him from the evil that will gather around his way in life, and see that through no fault of yours he miss the way to these heavenly mansions."

The mother clasped her baby to her heart in a wild pressure of joy, and then handing him back, said,

"No — no — no! That is too fearful to think of! Thanks to God he is safe — safe!"

And Lucy awoke.

"Yes, thank God he is safe!" trembled on her lips as consciousness grew clear.

"Mother, dear!" It was the soft, girlish voice of Lucy. Mrs. Wayland started from her dream, and looked at her in bewilderment for some moments.

"You have been asleep," said Lucy.

"Yes, love; but I am awake now."

She meant more than her words conveyed to Lucy, as the reader may believe. "If Mary had not died!" never again parted her lips in murmuring rebellion against that wise and good Providence without which not a sparrow falls.

X.

OUR DAILY BREAD.

DEAR little Charley! His thought seems always to rise above the visible and tangible. He is my teacher, often, in that wisdom which is not of this world. He sat very still in his chair, this morning, after family worship. I looked at his sober countenance, and wondered what could be passing in his busy little brain.

"Mother!" He was by my side, gazing up into my face.

"Well, dear?"

"What kind of bread is daily bread?"

"Bread," I answered, "means all kinds of nourishing food that give life to our bodies."

"Then why do we pray for it every morning? Our

bread, and meat, and sugar, and coffee, are all in the house before we pray." Charley looked puzzled.

"True, dear," I said; "but in thus praying, we acknowledge our dependence on God, who is the Giver of all good. It is his rain and sunshine that make the fields fruitful."

"Don't it mean something else, mother? Isn't there some other kind of bread?"

I looked down into dear Charley's eyes. There was a holy mystery in their crystalline, yet unfathomable depths. Something else? Another kind of bread? O yes; it did mean something else. There was another kind of bread. But I did not always think of this.

"We have souls as well as bodies," said I. A flush of interest went over his face. He leaned up closer to me. I saw deeper down into the mystery of his eyes; yet were they still unfathomable.

"There is a life of the soul, or spirit, as well as a life of the body." I saw that he comprehended me. "And to feed these two lives, there must be two kinds of food — natural food and spiritual food; food for the body and food for the soul."

"Is that the bread of heaven we read about in the Bible?" asked Charley.

"Yes, dear; the food on which angels live."

"And will God give us angels' food, when we ask

for our daily bread?" His eyes brightened, and a sunbeam shone out from his soul through the transparent tissues of his face.

"The Lord has said: Ask, and it shall be given you," was the reply that came, spontaneously, to my lips. He sat very still and quiet for several minutes; then shut his eyes, while a look of heavenly trust and sweetness pervaded his face. His lips moved; I bent my ear to listen, and the words fell from them like incense —

"Give us this day our daily bread."

I would have caught and hugged him to my heart; but dared not disturb the holy state of innocent faith in God. I did what was better; offered up the same prayer, and in the same spirit — thinking of food for the soul, instead of food for the body — angels' food.

On that morning I had risen with a heavy pressure over my left eye, and a dim sense of floating in my brain — the two well-known precursors of a sick headache, and consequent day of nervous irritation, disability and trial. Much more did I stand in need of spiritual than of natural food; of the bread that endureth unto eternal life, than of the bread that perisheth in the using. Never before, with so clear a comprehension of its higher meaning, had I asked for daily bread; for that spiritual food, by the nourishing power of which I was to have strength to do my duty.

I kissed my darling boy with a tenderer kiss than I had left there for a long time, and arose to take up my burden of care and work for the day. I needed all that higher strength for which I had prayed.

There are days in our life, in which it seems that everything gets at cross purposes; and this was one of them for me. My sick headache increased with its slow but steady accumulations of pain, rendering me more fitted for bed than for the duties that were before me.

"I don't want to go to school." The words smote on my ear, and sent a throb to my sensitive brain; for I understood too well the trouble that was at hand. My little daughter Mary fell, sometimes, into perverse humors; and this morning the evil spirits of resistance and disobedience had found a way of entrance into her heart. Her "I don't want to go to school," meant that she didn't intend going, unless forced to do so. Nothing short of actual punishment had usually prevailed with her on these occasions. For a few moments an impulse of anger blinded me. It was on my lips to say, in a sternly commanding voice —

"Well, you'll have to go, Miss!" But I checked the words. A thought of Charley, and the daily bread for which we had prayed, flashed through my mind, and I lifted my heart to God with a new repetition of my want, clothed in ideas of higher signification. I asked for spiritual strength in my time of trial; for all that I needed to give me power for right action. What a calm fell instantly on my spirit. The hard, passionate state passed; and I felt tender and loving toward my self-willed child. Taking her by the hand, I said, in a low, quiet voice —

"Mary, dear."

She lifted her eyes to mine with a sudden glance of inquiry. The petulance and resistance were already beginning to die around her mouth. I sat down, still holding her by the hand.

"Put your fingers there, dear." And I laid them against my left temple.

"Press hard, dear."

She pressed her small hand against the throbbing artery that lies there close upon the surface.

"Do you feel it beat?"

"Yes, mother."

"Every pulse, my child, that lifts itself against your finger, is for me a stroke of pain."

"O, mother." Pity and sympathy were in her gentle face.

"I have a sick headache to-day."

"I'm so sorry." And she kissed me lovingly. I returned the kiss, and then said —

"Get ready for school, dear, as quietly as possible; and be a good little girl. Every noise or trouble disturbs me this morning, and makes my head ache worse."

She kissed me again, repeating, "I'm so sorry;" and then got ready for school, and went off without a murmur.

"Give us this day our daily bread," came almost tearfully from my heart, in a thankful acknowledgment for strength received, and in prayer for coming needs.

Ill-natured complaints, and irritating neglects from domestics, came next in my round of trials. Dear Charley was by my side, a sweet reminder of duty. The prayer for daily bread went up from my heart; and the answer came in strength to do and say the right. I was able to possess my soul in peace.

Something went wrong with my husband. He came home at dinner-time with a frown on his face. He scarcely looked at me when he came in, and hardly spoke to the children. I had been at some pains to prepare him a favorite dish; and knew that it was nicer than usual. But he eat of it without a remark, and pushed his plate from him after he had finished, with an air of indifference that hurt and annoyed me. I was on the point of saying something that would, I doubt not, have provoked a wounding answer, when a glance at Charley's face, and a thought of my morning's experiences, kept back the words.

"He wants other food than that," I said within myself, "for his nourishment and sustenance to-day; the daily bread of which dear Charley spoke."

How instantly did all my feelings change toward him. The selfish annoyance and hardness went out of my heart. I said —

"Lord, give him the daily bread for which his soul is hungering; the strength he needs in trial."

His eyes turned, as if moved by some sudden impulse, to my face.

"You look pale," he said, kindly. "Are you not well?"

"Not very well. This is one of my sick headache days." I had to speak low to keep my voice steady. Tears were coming into my eyes; and I could not hold them back.

My husband glanced at his empty plate, and then to the dish from which he had helped himself in silence. I knew what was in his thoughts.. His better man had been restored.

"You should not have done this," he said. "But you are always so thoughtful."

He arose from the table; came round to where I sat,

and laying his hand over my hot temples, drew my head back against his bosom, and kissed me. I shut my eyes to hold in the tears; but they ran down over my cheeks, and I felt my lips quivering. But I was happy. Oh, very happy; and in thankfulness of heart sent up the prayer — "Lord, evermore give us this bread."

XI.

ALWAYS IN SUNSHINE.

THERE are men who always come to you in sunshine; and there are men whose presence you feel as a shadow. It is ever so, meet them when and where you will — at home, in the street, on 'Change, in the store, office, or counting-room — there is ever the radiant sunshine or the projected shadow.

As men are, so, in the main, will you find their homes. The man who turns his face always to the light brings his warm and genial sphere into his home-circle; while the man whose back is to the sun never enters the door of his dwelling without throwing a shadow over the household.

My Uncle Florian was a man whose spirit seemed to know perpetual sunshine. I never saw a cloud in his face; I never knew his coming to shadow the heart of even a little child. Dear Uncle Florian! What a rare pleasure it was when, leave obtained, I turned my steps lightly from the shadowed house where my early years were spent, and came, for a brief season, into the brightness of thy beloved presence!

"Ah! Hattie dear, is this you?" Memory will never lose the echo of his pleasant voice as he greeted my coming; nor do I feel the pressure of his hand lighter now upon my head than it was thirty years ago, when it buried itself among the golden curls of childhood.

My aunt was not so cheerful in spirit as Uncle Florian. She was more inclined to look upon the dark side of things, and to prophecy evil instead of good. But Uncle Florian never permitted the clouds to darken the whole sweep of her horizon. If he could not always scatter the leaden mass of vapor he would break it into rifts, and let in, here and there, broad strips of sunshine.

Children are always children — thoughtless, given to fits of passion, disobedient in little things, inclined to selfishness. I give the picture's shadowed side. My cousins were no exception. Children are not born angels; they come to us in the natural plane of life, and receive by inheritance natural inclinations, which unhappily, ever show a downward proclivity. But the germs of angelic life are in the inmost of their being, and the wise parent gives loving yet earnest heed to the insemination of these, which is done by the awakening of gentle, tender, unselfish affections, and the storing up of good and true principles in the mind.

My cousins were like other children; and their mother, like too many mothers, weakly indulgent at times, and passionate, unreasonable, and exacting at other times. Ill health — the curse of American mothers — made her often fretful, and dimmed her vision when she looked out upon life.

I remember one June day that I spent, as a great privilege, at Uncle Florian's. I did not ask of my father the privilege, for I feared his universal "No." But after he had gone forth, I enticed, with childish art, my weak, unhappy mother into consent. Quietly, almost demurely, fearing to show any exuberant feelings, I stole out from my shadowed home; and when once fairly beyond the gate, and across the road into the green fields, I flew over the intervening distance with the tremulous joy of an uncaged bird.

"Ah, Hattie, dear!" It was the kind voice of Uncle Florian. I met him at the gate, surrounded by my cousins. He laid his hand upon my head as usual, and stooped to receive my kiss.

"How are father and mother?"

"Well, I thank you."

Ah, but it was not well with them. Why, in my childish ignorance, I knew not. But, somehow, my father always came to us in shadow. His presence hushed the sports of his children. Our home rarely knew the blessing of cheerful sunshine.

"Take good care of Hattie, dears," said Uncle Florian, with a beaming countenance, as he turned from the gate; "and make this day in her life's calendar a golden one.

And it was a golden one, as were all the days I ever spent at Uncle Florian's. Yet was not the day all cloudless. It was more shadowed, perhaps, than any day I had ever spent with my cousins, who were, as I have said, like other children, given to fits of passion, and swayed by the sudden impulse of selfish feelings. Several times Aubry, the oldest of my cousins, who seemed for awhile possessed with a teasing spirit, worried his gentle sister Marion into tears, and sadly marred our pleasure. He would not go away and find his own enjoyment, but kept with us nearly all the morning, for no other reason, it seemed, than to gratify an unamiable temper.

At dinner-time — Uncle Florian had gone to the city, and would not return until towards evening — Marion complained bitterly of Aubry's conduct, and my aunt scolded sharply. The boy did not receive his mother's intemperately spoken reproof in a very good spirit, and was sent from the table in consequence of a disrespectful word dropped thoughtlessly from his lips — a word repented as soon as uttered, and which a wiser reproof on his mother's part would not have provoked.

I tasted no more food after Aubry was sent from the table.

"Your father shall hear of this!" said my aunt sternly, as Aubry left the room.

My cousin did not trouble us again during the remainder of the day. I met him several times, but he did not look cheerful. His own thoughts were, I saw, punishing him severely. A restless spirit kept him wandering about, and doing all kinds of out of the way things. Now you would see him turning the grindstone vigorously, though no one held axe or knife-blade upon the swiftly revolving periphery: now he was on the top of a hay-mow; now climbing the long, straight pole that bore up the painted bird-box, to see if the twittering swallow had laid an egg; and now lying upon the grass in restless indolence.

Crash! What is that? The boy had found his way out upon the branch of one of his father's choice plum trees, which had only this year come into bearing, and was laden with its first offerings of half-ripe fruit. His weight proved too heavy for the slender limb, and now, torn from his hold upon the tree, it lay in ruin upon the ground.

Aubry was unhurt. In falling he had alighted upon his feet. But if his body had escaped without harm, not so his mind; for he comprehended in an instant the extent of injury sustained by his father's favorite tree — a tree to which two years of careful attention had been given, and to the ripening of whose choicely flavored fruit that father had looked with so much pleasure. The shape of the tree was also a matter of pride with Uncle Florian. He had pruned it for two seasons with a careful attention to symmetry as well as fruit-bearing, and I had more than once heard him speak of its almost perfect form.

Tears were in the eyes of my cousin Aubry as we came up to where he stood gazing sadly upon the broken limb. My aunt had heard the crash and fall, and came running out from the house with a frightened air. The moment she comprehended the nature of what had occurred she struck her hands together passionately, and stung the already suffering mind of the boy with sharp, reproving words. Aubry made no answer. The pain he felt was too severe to find much accession from this cause; though any added pang was cruelty, no matter from what source it came.

"If it had been any other tree," said Aubry. I was sitting by his side, trying to comfort him, an hour after the accident. "If it had been any other tree I would not have cared so much. But father valued this one so highly. It was his favorite tree.

"He will not be angry." I was thinking how very angry my own father would have been under like circumstances, and how severely he would have punished my brother had he been guilty of a similar fault. "He is always so cheerful — always so ready to forgive."

"It isn't that, cousin Hattie — it isn't that," answered the boy, in a troubled voice. "It is not his anger I fear."

"What, then, have you to fear?" I inquired.

"His sorrow, cousin. Ah, Hattie! that is worse than his anger. He took so much pride in this tree; and now it is ruined forever!"

"Only a single limb is broken. The tree is not destroyed. There is much fruit on it still," I said trying to comfort him.

"It's beauty is gone," replied Aubry. "That beauty which father produced by such careful pruning. No, Hattie; there is no bright side to the picture. All is dark."

It was in vain; we could not comfort the unhappy boy, who spent the rest of the day alone, brooding over the event which had so troubled his peace.

"There's your father," I heard my aunt say, a little before sundown. She was speaking to Aubry, and her voice had in it neither encouragement nor comfort. The breaking of the tree had excited her anger, and she still felt something of unkindness. I looked from the window and saw Uncle Florian alighting from his horse. His face was turned towards us — his kind, good face, that always looked as if the sun were shining upon it. Aubry arose — he had been sitting by a table, with a dejected air, his head resting upon his hand — and went out hastily to meet his father.

"I hope," said my aunt, "that he will give him a good scolding; he richly deserves it. What business had he to climb into that tree, and out upon so slender a limb?"

I felt an almost breathless interest in the meeting between my cousin and Uncle Florian. I had never seen that mild face clouded, but I was sure it would be clouded now. How could it help being? His countenance as he stood with his hand resting upon the neck of his horse, was still turned towards us, and I could see every varying expression. My breathing was nearly suspended as I saw Aubry reach his father and look up into his face. A little while he talked to him, while Uncle Florian listened attentively. Every instant I expected to see the cloud, but it came not to dim the light of cheerful kindness in that almost angelic countenance. While Aubry yet talked, earnestly, to his father, one of the farm hands came out from the stable and took the horse. Then the two — father and son — came towards the house; and as the former commenced speaking, in answer to the communication which he had received, I noticed that he laid his hand upon the shoulder of Aubry in an affectionate way, and drew him close to his side. They passed near the broken plum tree, but neither looked at it. I think Uncle Florian avoided a sight which, just then, could hardly have been without an unpleasant shock to his feelings.

Now, as ever, dear Uncle Florian came in sunshine; and it was warm enough and bright enough to chase away coldness and shadow even from the heart and brow of my aunt, who could not forgive the offence of her boy.

For every one my good uncle had a smile or a pleasant word. If in degree there was a difference, it was in favor of Aubry, who seemed held to his father's side by some irresistible attraction. Instead of separating between him and his father, I think that little unpleasant event drew them nearer together, and bound their hearts closer by the magic tie of love.

As I turned my face homeward that evening I felt that I had turned it away from the sunshine; and so it was. A trifling fault of one of my brothers had been visited by excessive punishment, given in anger, and there was gloom in the household — and not only gloom, but alienation, the germ of separation.

We were sitting, the next morning, at our late, silent, moody breakfast — silent and moody after rebuking words from my father, who seemed only half satisfied with the punishment already meted out to my brother — when the door opened, and a cheerful voice sent a chord of pleasant music vibrating through the room, and a face that always came in sunshine scattered, with its golden beams, the clouds which curtained all our feelings. Smiles warmed over the sober face of my mother, and light sparkled in her eyes, while the whole aspect of my father's countenance underwent a change.

"Ah, Harry!" Uncle Florian spoke to my brother, who was in disgrace for a fault light in every way compared to the fault of Aubry on the day previous, "how finely you are growing! Really, you are the handsomest boy in the neighborhood."

"If he were only as good as he is good looking," said my mother.

"Tut! tut!" replied Uncle Florian, half aside, to my mother. "Never say that to a boy's face." Then aloud and cheerfully, "I'll stand sponsor for Harry, and put his good conduct against his good looks any day." What a grateful expression my brother cast upon him.

For each and all Uncle Florian had a kind word, and upon each and all fell the warm sunlight of his cheerful spirit. When he left us, after his brief visit, we were all happier. Even my father's brows were less contracted, and his voice was kinder when he spoke; and as for my mother, her heart was warmer and her countenance brighter through all the day that followed.

Blessings on Uncle Florian, and all men who, like him, come to us in sunshine! They carry their own heaven with them, and give to every one they meet a glimpse of its sweet beatitudes. Ever more ready to praise than blame — to see good rather than evil — to find the sunny instead of the cloudy side — they are like the angels of whom it has been said, that when they come to a man they search only for what is good in him, that they may warm the celestial seed into germination, knowing that if the forces of life are directed into the good seed the evil must lie dormant. Long years since he went to his rest — his days declining, like the last warm days of the later autumn, and his western sky radiant with the passing glories of a spirit that always clothed itself in sunbeams.

XII.

MRS. GOLDSMITH AT FORTY.

HE case of Mrs. Goldsmith was a sad one. I did not see the remedy. She was forty, and not so happy as at thirty-five. At thirty, her face, though beginning to look at times dreamy and discontented, was for the most part bright with anticipation. Her three children, all daughters, were unfolding from bud to fragrant blossom, and her life rested in their lives.

Since the completion of her thirty-fifth year one of her children had died — the youngest and most tenderly loved because the youngest. Ah! for a woman like Mrs. Goldsmith, who had built only on an earthly foundation, who had loved herself intensely in her children, this was indeed an affliction. She bowed her head, and refused to be comforted. The unrelieved black that gathered in funereal gloom around her person was a fitting emblem of the darkness that enshrouded her spirit. But troubles and sorrows do not always come alone. Her oldest daughter formed an attachment that did not meet her parents' approbation; and failing to gain their consent, or even the smallest approval of her choice, took the desperate and almost always unwise course of marrying against their remonstrances, threats, and commands. From the day she left her father's house she had been an alien therefrom; and two long years had passed without a reconciliation.

So at forty Mrs. Goldsmith had cause of mental suffering and heart-disquietude; but the suffering and disquietude were in excess of legitimate causes. The home of Mrs. Goldsmith was luxurious. So far as her external life was concerned, or rather, so far as in the use of money she could arrange the externals of her life, she had all the means of happiness; but these, in her case were wholly inadequate. Nay, instead of giving that repose of mind which freedom from worldly anxieties is supposed to confer, they only add to her dissatisfaction. Their possession brought no sense of responsibility, but induced a feeling of superiority to others. She must always be ministered to, never minister. Her comforts, feelings, tastes, habits, desires, and conveniences must be regarded by her domestics and by all from whom she required service in any thing; while to their feelings, tastes, habits, and conveniences no regard was ever paid. Her position of luxurious ease had made her, as it does so many in like situations, intensely selfish — and this very selfishness was a cause of her miserable disquietude.

Mortified pride was another source of unhappiness in the case of Mrs. Goldsmith. To think that *her* daughter should humiliate the family by marrying beneath their condition! Death, fearful as the visitation had been, was a light affliction compared with this, and disturbed not half so profoundly.

Poor Mrs. Goldsmith! At forty, as I have said, her case was a sad one, and I did not see the remedy. Human efforts to bring her mind back into the sunshine were of no avail. She brooded over her sorrow and her humiliation, admitting no cheerful guests into her heart. Mortification at her daughter's discreditable marriage, added to a morbid grief — half affected, half real — that succeeded the first strong outgush of maternal anguish, caused an entire withdrawal of herself from society, and shut her up in the shadowy retirement of her own chamber for a greater portion of the time.

No interest for others could be awakened in the mind of Mrs. Goldsmith. What was the outside world to her? Human sympathy was barred from her heart. She felt herself to be of finer quality than the mass of people around her; and in her sorrow and stricken pride she held herself coldly aloof.

If Mrs. Goldsmith had taken interest in any employment — had gone down, with a true woman's care and thought, into her household, and wrought out therein the highest possible comfort for its inmates — then would she have found seasons of calmness and peace. But instead of this, neglect and indifference produced constant irregularities; and sharp, angry, or injudicious reproof and complainings alienated domestics, and made the home of Mrs. Goldsmith so unlike a true home that it scarcely deserved the name.

And so life at forty was proving a failure to one whose promise at twenty appeared bright as a cloudless day in June. I called one evening to see her husband — a man of large business operations, whose sober, abstracted face did not indicate a peaceful mind. Care drew tightly on the muscles about his lips, wrinkled his forehead, and fixed his eyes in an absent kind of gaze, as if he were looking away from the present into some far beyond. It was not often that visitors saw Mrs. Goldsmith. I was privileged. She did not retire from the family circle on my entrance. A fleeting smile lit up her pale face as I came in; but it faded quickly, leaving a weary, desolate look in her eyes and about her mouth. Her conversation was as dreary as her face.

Domestic troubles — the worthlessness of servants — the daily and hourly vexations to which the family were subjected — poor health — depression of spirits — these were the topics dwelt upon during the hour I staid. I tried several times to get her mind away from them — to interest her in other people or other themes; but, like a strained spring, it came always back to its common adjustment.

"The case of Mrs. Goldsmith is hopeless," I said to myself on retiring. "What are wealth and luxury worth if their possessors can use them to no better advantage than this? Inaction produces stagnation, and stagnation breeds sickly forms of life. The mind of Mrs. Goldsmith is a stagnant pool. Miasma hangs over the surface like a cold vapor, and in the sluggish waters below monstrous creatures are taking shape and vitality. Storm and flood were better than this! Let the pool be swept in ruin away, so that even the tiniest stream remain, singing, as its pure waters flow on and on, its happy song, chording sweetly with every wind-note that kisses the flower-heads bending above! Yes, yes; this were better far."

A year afterward, in a distant city, I read of Mr. Goldsmith's sudden death; and letters received from home soon afterward gave me the information that he died a bankrupt. "His widow is left without a dollar," was the language of my correspondent.

"Poor Mrs. Goldsmith!" said I, looking up from my letter, and recalling her image as last seen. "Here is trouble indeed! — trouble that you can not sit down and brood over — trouble that will give no permission for an elegant retirement from the world — trouble that neither pride nor a selfish love of ease can nurture. Ah! is there any strength left for an ordeal like this? Will gold be found in the crucible after the fire has reached its intensest heat?"

After an absence of three years I returned. In my own absorbing duties — in my own trials, sufferings, and life-discipline — Mrs. Goldsmith was forgotten, or only remembered at times with a vague impersonality. She was of the great outside world of men and women who do not touch the chords of an individual life, nor awaken a sympathetic interest.

I was sitting in one of the parlors of an old and valued friend when a young lady, who had rung at the door and been admitted by the servant, came in. My friend said, in a kind, familiar voice, but without introducing her,

"Oh, Margaret!"

"Miss Annie is at home?" There was a low, pleasant tone in the speaker's voice.

"Yes. Walk into the back parlor. She'll be with you in a moment."

The young lady passed through the folding-doors, and we were alone again.

"There's something familiar in her face," said I, looking inquiringly at my friend.

"Anna's music-teacher; a Miss Goldsmith."

"Not the daughter of Robert Goldsmith, who died a few years ago?"

"Yes."

"What of her mother?" I asked, with a suddenly-quickened interest. "Is she living?"

"Oh yes."

"Where, and how?"

"With her daughter."

"Whom she cast off in anger on account of her marriage with a young man regarded as beneath her?"

"Yes."

"What of him?" I inquired.

"He's an estimable person, I believe, and holds a responsible position in one of our large mercantile houses."

"What a blow to pride! I wonder how Mrs. Goldsmith's present state compares with her condition of mind when she stood in the higher ranks?"

But my friend could not answer the question. She had not known Mrs. Goldsmith in the days of her prosperity, and only knew of her now through her daughter, who came twice a week to give music lessons.

Next morning I called upon my old acquaintance, now in adversity. Nearly ten minutes passed after sending up my card before she made her appearance. I began to have misgivings as to the state in which I should find her.

A rustling of garments on the stairs — the pleasant pattering of little feet — the music of a child's questioning voice — and then Mrs. Goldsmith entered, leading a golden-haired little girl of some three summers by the hand. One glance into her pale, calm, humanized face told the story of suffering and triumph. She had been down among the seething waters of sorrow and adversity, but had risen above them in the strength of a nobler and purer love than had burned in her heart in the days of wealth and luxurious ease.

"It was kind in you to call," she said as she stood holding my hand and looking at me with a gratified expression on her face.

"I am grieved," I said, using the common form of expression, "to find that since my absence from the city sad changes have met you."

She smiled faintly as she answered, "God's ways are not as our ways."

"But His ways are always best," I said, quickly.

"Always — always," she replied, the smile growing sweeter about her mouth.

"Though our feet turn to them unwillingly," I remarked.

"Very unwillingly, as in my case."

We were seated. The sunny-haired child was in her arms, her head laid back, and her eyes turned lovingly upward. Mrs. Goldsmith looked down upon the sweet face, and left a kiss upon it.

"Your grand-daughter?"

"Yes, and she's a darling little girl!" Her arms, on which the child lay, felt the loving impulse that was in her heart, and drew the form close against her breast. I noticed the movement, and said, in my thought, "Yes; His ways are best — always — always."

"There has been much lost," she said, in the earnest talk that followed — "much lost, and much gained; and the gain is greater than the loss. Oh, into what a blind, selfish, sinful state had I fallen when that sterner visitation and discipline came, and I sunk for a time in utter despair. Then I became conscious that a struggle for very life had come, and that not only for myself, but for another also — a struggle in which victory would be reached only in the degree that I had in myself the elements of strength. In the wreck of my husband's estate every thing was lost. Our elegant home and luxurious furniture receded from possession, fading away, in our bewilderment and grief, like a dissolving view, or the passing of scenery in a play. My first distinct impression was like that of a man in the midst of overwhelming waters, and I began reaching about fearfully, in my thought, for a way of safety and escape. Then the despised and contemned one — he from whom we had turned ourselves away in bitter scorn — came and spoke such kind, true, tender, and manly words, that my rebuked and smitten heart bowed itself before him in something of reverence. I saw in what loving trust and confidence my daughter leaned upon him, secure and steadfast, while against me and my other child the floods swept fiercely, and it seemed as if no power could save us.

"Ah! Sir, God led us down into a deep, dark, frightful valley, only that he might show us the way to a mountain of love, rising heavenward, beyond. I could not go in through the door opened for us in such a manly, Christian spirit, and sit down in idleness, with folded hands. The generous conduct of my daughter's husband inspired me with a desire to return benefit for benefit, and though here, under the law of filial love, I try daily to let gratitude express itself in service; and so, in useful employments, I find a new life in which peace dwells. Margaret will not be idle and dependent. It is not the wish of her excellent brother-in-law that she should teach; but duty has led her into the right way, and she is cheerful and happy."

"Not in the external things of this life," I said, as she paused, "can the heart find rest."

"Nor without them," she replied. "We must make them the ministers of useful service; must dwell in them, as life dwells in true forms, directing and controlling them for those good uses they were intended to serve."

"Then," said I, "they will be as Aaron's rod in the hand — a staff for support; and not as Aaron's rod on the ground — a stinging serpent."

XIII.

A DAY'S EXPERIENCE.

"I don't know about that," said Mr. Dennison, as he lifted his eyes from the page he was reading, and remained for some time in a thoughtful position. "I don't know about that," and he looked upon the page again as he repeated the sentence, and read aloud: "A man who undertakes to make universal life serve him will always be aggrieved. 'It is more blessed to give than to receive;' and the man who, with loving zeal, goes out into life, giving his own soul to things about him, finds life easy, and rich, and full, and strong, while nobody else does."

Mr. Dennison, after puzzling himself for a little while over the suggestions which were born of the precept given above, dismissed the subject, and let the easier current of his thoughts flow on in its usual direction.

Out into the world Mr. Dennison passed, and for another day, entered into his work. He was an earnest man and a strong man, usually pressing to the accomplishment of his will, with a resolute purpose that swept aside all feebler resistances. But strong and earnest men are apt to come in contact with men as strong and earnest as themselves, and through these are repressed by limitations. None are permitted to work to the full accomplishment of their ends. Other interests are perpetually antagonizing them. And so it happens that those who undertake to make universal life serve them, are perpetually aggrieved.

Take a single day in the experience of Mr. Dennison. He was in position at an early business hour, all on the alert as usual. A man came into his store. He had been expecting him.

"Good morning, Mr. Henry," said he with a courteous smile.

Mr. Henry returned the salutation, but in slight embarrassment.

"I've only brought you three hundred dollars," said the latter.

"Ah! I'm sorry for that." And the light went out of Mr. Dennison's face. "I fully counted on six hundred."

"Not with more confidence than I counted on making up the sum. Here is all I can raise." And Mr. Henry placed a check in the hand of Mr. Dennison, who received it in a cold and ungracious manner.

"How soon can you make up the balance?" asked the latter, in a tone very different from that in which he had greeted his visitor a few moments before.

"I will endeavor to do so this week," said Mr. Henry, in a depressed voice.

There followed an unpleasant silence. Then Mr. Henry said "good morning," and retired.

Mr. Dennison had received three hundred dollars of a sum due him by a fellow merchant, and the promise of three hundred more in a week. He was in no fear of losing the balance due; but having expected to receive the full sum on that morning, he experienced a feeling of disappointment that led him to deal unkindly with a man who was already suffering because unable to keep his engagement.

A state of mind far from agreeable was the consequence of this incident. There were two causes of disquietude: a failure to receive an expected sum of money, which he purposed using to advantage, and a consciousness that he had wounded the feelings of a man to whom kind consideration should have been extended. There was an element of pleasure in that incident, but

Mr. Dennison had failed to extract it. If he could so far have forgotten himself as to feel pity for his neighbor's troubled state of mind, and met his declared inability to fulfill an engagement with cheerful acquiescence, that self-denial would have been followed by an interior satisfaction strongly in contrast with the disquietude that actually came.

Mr. Dennison was not made stronger for the day's assaults upon his peace of mind by this opening incident. He was fully committed to self-service, and his soul cried into the world, "Give! Give!" with an undying eagerness. The day was to be his own, and every act for himself. Not a pulse beat in harmony with the common pulse; not a thought embraced his neighbor.

"I've closed that bargain," said a man, who entered Mr. Dennison's store soon after Mr. Henry's departure.

"You have!" There was surprise in Mr. Dennison's voice, and a falling of his countenance.

"Yes; you held your lot too firmly. I was certain, as I told you yesterday, that I could do better with Raynor."

"I might have receded. Why didn't you come to me before closing with Raynor?" said Mr. Dennison.

"You were decided about the matter when I was here last."

"True; but I wished to sell, and if I had supposed,

for an instant, that Raynor would have given away," — Mr. Dennison checked himself, and tried to rally and assume an air of indifference. But his disappointment was too great. The lot of ground which he had failed to sell, was one that he was desirous of exchanging for money, and for which, at any time during the past two years, he would have sold for twenty per cent. less than the price just asked of a man who wanted it for a particular purpose. In his eagerness to get the highest possible price, Mr. Dennison had overreached himself, and chagrin was added to his disappointment.

"I'm sorry," remarked his visitor, with a shade of regret in his voice. "Your lot would have suited me better; but the price at which I bought was a consideration."

"What are you to pay Raynor?" asked Mr. Dennison.

"Two thousand three hundred dollars."

"Mine is the most desirable for your purpose."

"Yes."

"You shall have it for the same."

But the man shook his head, saying; "The transaction is closed. I have agreed to take Mr. Raynor's lot."

"But I want you to have my lot. It will answer your purpose a great deal better than Raynor's. Take it for two thousand two hundred dollars."

Mr. Dennison, in his eagerness to dispose of his property, was losing sight of honor.

"Sir," answered his visitor, with some sternness of manner, "I never forfeit my word."

"Why do you say that?" Mr. Dennison colored.

"I told you the transaction was closed; that I had agreed to take Raynor's lot."

"Oh, so you did! Excuse me. I did not rightly consider your word."

Mr. Dennison's face wore a sober aspect after the visitor had retired. The incident had hurt him considerably — hurt his self-esteem as well as his cupidity. In attempting to get the utmost farthing possible in a transaction with his neighbor, he had lost the sale of property on which he was yearly sinking interest and taxes; and lost also his own self-respect and the good opinion of this neighbor. These were not circumstances favorable to mental tranquility.

In the ordinary business transactions of the day, many things occurred to fret and chafe the mind of Mr. Dennison. Scarcely anything came out just right. Not a sale was made in which the satisfaction arising from a consideration of the profit, was not marred by regret that the benefit to himself was not larger. In fact, results were all the while falling below desires. Nearly every thought and act were limited to the narrow circumference of his own little world of self. He demanded service of every thing and every body, and every thing and every body that served him, did so with stint and reluctance.

And so it happened in Mr. Dennison's case, as it happens with such men, that results in life were always inadequate. Nothing came out just right; nothing accomplished gave the hoped-for tranquillity and satisfaction. Self-seeking cursed itself perpetually.

Mr. Dennison sat, towards mid-day, revolving some scheme of profit in his mind, when a lad came in and handed him a letter. He broke the seal and read:

"DEAR SIR—I am anxious to get my son Charles, who will hand you this, into some business where he can earn a few dollars weekly. My circumstances, I regret to say, are greatly reduced, rendering some employment on the part of my boy necessary. Will you do for me what you can? Very respectfully, MARGARET WISTAR."

The reading of this letter threw something of a chill over the feelings of Mr. Dennison. Mrs. Wistar was the widow of an old friend, with whom he had once been on terms of close intimacy; he could not, therefore, treat her application with entire indifference; but how was he to turn aside from busy self-service to serve another? The application seemed altogether out of place. Twice he read the letter over, and then, in forced consideration for the lad, looked coldly upon him, and said:

"You are Mrs. Wistar's son?"

"Yes, sir." The boy felt the merchant's repellant sphere like a hand pushing him away

"What can you do?"

"I could stand in a store, sir, or run of errands. I'm willing to do anything, sir."

"Hum—m. I don't know of any place. It's been a bad season just now. But, tell your mother that I'll bear it in mind, and see what can be done."

The boy shrunk away, feeling but little encouraged by Mr. Dennison's coldly uttered promise. He was scarcely twenty paces from the merchant's desk, when his mother's letter was carelessly thrown aside.

But Mr. Dennison could not, as carelessly, put aside the thought of Mrs. Wistar. Old incidents and relations connected with the former life, revived in his memory, rebuking indifference, and compelling him to regard her application as having something of a blinding force.

"I can't do anything for the boy," he said, half-fretfully, to himself, trying to get away from convictions of duty. But these convictions were not to be set aside, and they kept haunting him until thought turned from his own affairs, and he gave a brief interval of precious time to the lad. In that brief interval the right suggestion came.

"I will see about it at once," said Mr. Dennison, taking up his hat and going out. There was a pleasant exhilaration in his thoughts. He was successful. In less than an hour from the time Charles Wistar left his store, feeling that no good would come from the application, his mother received an answer to her letter, conveying the gratifying intelligence that an excellent place had been secured for her son.

On the evening of that day, Mr. Dennison sat musing, as was his wont, over the day's results. He was in a more satisfied state of mind than usual, and, strange as it seemed to him, on tracing this feeling to its source it was not connected with any good accomplished for himself, but came from the good deed done for Mrs. Wistar. He had gained liberally in more than one transaction; had reached certain desirable ends; yet, in all that was of self, a certain disquietude and dissatisfaction were connected — while his thoughts of the widow and her son gave an unalloyed pleasure.

As he mused over the day's doings, a note was placed in his hands.

"DEAR SIR — Your prompt kindness has touched my heart. I did not say how pressing was my extremity. But that you may know the great service you have rendered, I will declare the truth. If Charles had not obtained employment, I should have been forced to break up my little family. But the bond is not yet loosened, thank God! May heaven bless you, as it will!

Gratefully,
Margaret Wistar."

A little while afterwards, Mr. Dennison took up the volume from which he had read a few sentences in the morning, and the same passages met his eyes. He let them come into his thoughts again: — "Some men go around saying to things, 'Why don't you serve me? Why don't you please me?' They are forever complaining that nothing helps them, and that everything is against them. A man that undertakes to make universal life serve him, will always be aggrieved. It is more blessed to give than to receive; and the man that with loving zeal goes out into life, giving his soul to things about him, finds life easy, and rich, and full, and strong, while nobody else does."

Did he say, as in the morning, "I don't know about that?" Not so; but, with a dawning perception of a great truth, spoke thus with himself: "Life's best philosophy is doubtless embodied here. I must ponder these things. In what I have gained for self to-day, no true pleasure has been born; while that one good deed fills my heart with a glow of satisfaction."

XIV.

JUST BEYOND.

WE heard, or dreamed, this story of two lost children, a boy and a girl. They had gone for an afternoon's berrying in the fields and woods, and after filling their baskets, started for home. But the sky had become heavily overcast with clouds, so that they couldn't tell the east from the west; and as they had wandered away from old beaten paths, and familiar localities, the effort to reach their home ere nightfall proved fruitless. With blank, pale face, and lips trembling with fear, the youngest, a boy, looked up to his companion, as the evening shadows began to creep down among the thick leaved branches of the trees, and said,

"Oh, sister Edie! Are we lost?"

Edie did not answer; but the boy saw the paleness of his own face reflected in her's.

"This is the way, I think."

She did not feel the confidence which she sought to throw into her voice; but she was one year older than her brother, and must, therefore, act for both. She felt the flutter of his hand, as it clung to her's tightly.

But the little opening among the trees toward which she hurried, terminated, at the end of a hundred yards, in a dense mass of underwood, through which she did not venture to go.

"Are we lost, sister?" again asked the other child.

"It can't be far from home, Willie. We'll soon find our way out of the woods. Don't cry!"

A sob, and then a wail of fear cut the still air.

"Don't cry. We'll soon be home."

How bravely Edie tried to speak, even while her own heart was sinking. The boy hid his face against her, weeping and shuddering. He had heard about children being lost in the woods, and terror overcame him.

Half forgetting herself, in pity for her affrighted and almost helpless brother, Edie grew brave and strong, instead of cowardly and weak.

"Crying don't do any good, Willie," she spoke in a firm tone; "and we'll never get home if we stand still."

She moved back the way she had come through the opening among the trees, holding Willie by the hand.

"This is the way. I know it now." She spoke with more confidence than she felt. Cattle tracks were seen, and she followed them down into deep ravines, along hillside, across narrow clearing, and then into a dense wood, where she lost them in the darkness of coming night — and stood still trembling.

Willie's cries broke out again. He was in despair.

"Hark!" said Edie.

The two children listened.

"What did you hear, Edie?"

The child's voice was unnatural and choking.

"Listen! That's a dog, Willie! That's our Lion."

"I don't hear any dog, Edie."

"But I do! Come! This is the way!" and Edie pulled Willie after her, through brush and briar, hastening in the direction from which, to her ears, had seemed to come the barking of a dog. Their hands and faces were scratched and their clothes torn — their limbs ached with fatigue — still they kept on, until the edge of the woods was reached, and they saw a wide field stretching beyond.

"It's only a little way now," said Edie, in a brave, confiding voice.

"But I'm so tired!" moaned Willie, dragging back, "and my foot hurts me."

"Hark! That's it again. That's Lion!"

"I don't hear any dog," answered Willie.

"But I do. Now, walk on briskly. Come, Willie."

Thus urged, the child kept on by the side of his sister, until half across the field; but, his chafed and smarting feet, his aching limbs, and his burden of fear were too much for endurance, and he stood still again, crying sadly.

"Our house is just beyond the hill, over the field, Willie. I heard Lion. Now do come along. It's getting so dark that we'll be lost, if we don't hurry."

"We're lost, now!" sobbed Willie. "O dear! O dear!" and he cried more distressingly.

"Listen!" said Edie.

Her brother ceased crying.

"What do you hear?"

"That was Lion, barking."

"I don't hear him."

"There! I hear it again. It's Lion. Come! Let's hurry across the field."

Thus urged, faint-hearted little Willie took courage again, and moved onward with his sister, though always a step behind. They were nearly across the field, when both stumbled over a sudden rise in the ground, and then fell forward into a ditch. Edie scrambled quickly to her feet, but Willie lay in helpless despair amid the water and mire. It took all the brave little girl's strength to drag him out, and over to the other side of the ditch, on to the firm dry ground. Here he lay down in utter abandonment, crying in a low, tremulous wail. Unmindful of her own condition, Edie took off Willie's shoes and poured out the water; then put them on again, and wiped, with handfuls of grass and leaves, the mud from his clothes, speaking all the while comforting and hopeful words. After a time, she persuaded him to walk forward again.

Over the field, into the skirting woods, and across the hill, beyond which Edie was certain their home lay; and yet, no human habitation came in sight. The children stood still and hearkened. In the hush of the gloomy woods, strange low sounds crept into their ears, and undefined terrors oppressed them. Haunting fears of wild beasts, or of savage men who delighted in cruelty and murder — they had read of such things in books — crowded upon their hearts. The courage and self-reliance which had, until now, sustained Edie, were about giving way, when Willie hid his face in her dress, and she felt the weight of his body leaning heavily against her, and its tremors running along her nerves. So, more for his sake than her own, she aroused herself, and with hopeful utterance, moved forward again, drawing him lagging, weary and sore-footed after her.

It was night now — moonless and starless night, and very dark. But in a little while the children came to an open road, cut with wagon-tracks. Then they took heart and walked on more quickly.

"We shall soon be home now," said brave, hopeful Edie.

"But you don't hear Lion any more," answered fearful, doubting Willie.

"Maybe he isn't barking; you know he does'nt bark all the while." That was for Willie's encouragement. His suggestion had shaken her confidence.

A weary half mile, and then Willie would go no farther. Fatigue and hopelessness had driven away the terrors with which darkness had at first oppressed him. It was all in vain that Edie coaxed, persuaded, promised, even scolded in simulated anger. He sat down on the roadside at the foot of a steep hill, and would not stir.

"I know it's just over the hill, Willie. Now do come a little further."

"You've kept saying that all the while," answered the boy, fretfully, "and I don't believe it any more."

And yet Edie was right this time. Home lay just beyond. One more effort — one more difficulty subdued — another weary hill ascended, and they would be in their father's house. But, Willie's faith, hope, endurance were all gone. No argument could move him, and no suggestion revive his dead confidence; even while Edie wrought with him he went fast asleep. Then it was that the sister's brave heart sunk down despairingly; that her cheeks, dry until now, reflected the star-light from great falling tears; that her sobs, long held back for Willie's sake, shook themselves free, and went forth in dissonant moans upon the air. Sitting down upon the roadside, with the woman's instinctive self-devotion still ruling in her young breast, Edie drew the head of her unconscious brother into her lap, and leaning her wet face down upon his, wept herself into oblivion.

Yet, just beyond, home awaited them! One more effort, and its gleaming windows would have gladdened their eyes. And, for lack of this, they went to sleep, as lost children, out in the cold night, exposed to harms. As the story goes — heard or dreamed, which it does not signify — a neighbor, returning late that way, found them on the roadside, and bore them in his stout arms home, where, when their senses woke with the awakening morning, they found themselves in safety.

Just beyond! Ah, how many, like these children, sit down despairing on the wayside, in some gloomy valley, with the goal for which they are striving over the next hill of difficulty, and just beyond. Fainting sojourner in the ways of life, never give up your confidence. If the night falls, and the path is lost, still keep a brave heart. Walk onward, warily, because of the darkness, yet ever onward — the good you seek; or, mayhap, a higher and more permanent good is beyond — just beyond for all you know, and about rewarding your toilsome efforts. The world is not all wilderness. Night ever gives way to morning. If there are steep and weary hills, there are also level plains and pleasant valleys. If in the forest, press on in courage and patience — you will find the open clearing. If the mountain looks rugged and high, and you are faint and weary, do not sit down in despair at the foot, but gird up your loins and pass to the other side. It may be the last mountain for many a mile, and smiling meadows may lie beyond. If you are lost in a bewildering maze of events which your dull eyes cannot read, still look upward and beyond, pressing forward, though your feet are sore and your tired limbs ache.

Just beyond! Just beyond! For lack of this faith, how many fall in their tracks, going to sleep, with no stout arms to lift them, as the slumbering children were lifted and borne forward to their home.

Never despair! If your motives are right — if, in the midst of errors, and even evils of life into which an evil heart may, when off your guard, have betrayed you, you are still conscious of good and true purposes toward all men; if your aspirations are for the better things of heaven, do not despair, though you cannot see a star in the clouded heavens, and no tracks on the ground show that feet have ever passed that way before. It happens to every one, at some period in his life, that he must go into the wilderness alone, and walk in personal experience, where none, but the Incarnate God, has walked before. But, God knows the way, and if you look to him and press onward, He will surely bring you out in safety. Oh, do not then despair; no matter how dark the night, how bewildered the way, how high the mountain, walk forward — home may be just beyond at the time you are in sorest doubt.

To all, whether in lowest or highest things, let the admonition come. Never faint, never falter, never abandon yourself to weak fears. In difficulty, in doubt, in danger, ever be on the alert, hopeful and on-pressing; success, accomplishment, home, are beyond, and to gain you must move forward — they must lie *just* beyond. Picture to your mind those lost children asleep in the valley, while just over the next hill top their home-lights stream from every inviting window; and if you are tempted to give up, like them, arouse yourself, and climb the difficult mountain that lies across your way. It may bring you to all you have striven for through years.

XV.

MORE BLESSED TO GIVE.

"MORE blessed to give than to receive."

It was the low, half-questioning voice of a child, whose thoughts went out into audible expression. "More blessed to give?" she repeated. "More blessed?"

And then she was silent again. She had been reading, and this divine truth falling into the rich, tender soil of her young mind, had already begun to germinate.

"Mother;" the child was now standing by her mother, and looking into her face, "Is it more blessed to give than to receive?"

"Yes, dear, far more blessed."

"What does it mean by being more blessed?" inquired the child.

"It means, that giving will make us happier than receiving."

"Then you and father will be happier to-morrow, than the rest of us; for you will make all the presents."

"Don't you intend making any presents, my love?" asked the mother.

"I never thought of that," answered the child. And then her countenance took on a more serious aspect.

"It is hardly fair that we should be happiest of all," said the mother.

"You are best of all, and should be happiest of all," replied little Ernestine, quickly.

The mother could not help kissing her child. She said, as she did so,

"We are happy in our children; and whatever increases their happiness, increases ours."

Ernestine looked down to the floor, and mused for some moments. The good seed was quickening into life.

"I have nothing to give." She looked up as she spoke, and there was a touch of regret in her voice.

"Think." It was all the mother said.

The child thought for some time.

"There is half a dollar in my saving's bank. But you know I'm going to buy a little sofa for my baby-house."

The door of the sitting-room opened, and a child came in with some coarse aprons and napkins which her mother had been making for the mother of Ernestine. Her clothes were poor, and not warm enough for the season, and she had on her head the wreck of an old bonnet that let in the wind at a dozen places. A few words passed between her and the lady, and then she went, with quiet steps, from the room. The eyes of Ernestine were fixed upon this child intently, while she remained; they followed her from the room, and rested upon the door some time after she had withdrawn. Her mother, who had become interested in the work brought home by the little girl, said nothing more to Ernestine, at the time, and so her thoughts were free to run their own way.

The evening which closed in that day, was the evening before Christmas.

"Where is Ernestine?"

It was the child's father who made the inquiry. He had returned home from his office a little earlier than usual, and before the twilight had given place to darkness.

"She was here a few minutes ago," replied the mother, and she lifted her voice, and called, "Ernestine!"

But there was no answer.

"Ernestine! Ernestine!"

Still no reply came.

"I wonder where she can be?"

While the question was yet on her lips, the street door opened, and the child came in, with hushed, gliding footsteps. She had a small package in her hands, which, on seeing her father and mother, she made an effort to conceal.

"Ah! Here is our pet!" said the father. "Why, darling, where have you been?"

There came a warm flush into the little one's face; and something of confusion showed itself in her manner.

"I know all about it," spoke up the mother, gaily.

"No you don't!" And Ernestine's face took on a serious aspect.

"Yes. It's the sofa for the baby-house."

"No." The flush came back to the child's fair brow.

Almost a minute of silence passed. It was a picture for a painter, that group. The child stood, half timid, half-irresolutely, with her eyes upon the floor, and her hands behind her, endeavoring to conceal the package she held; her parents looking at her in loving wonder. Slowly, at length, a hand came forward —

"What is it, darling?" The mother's voice had in it a slight flutter, for something of the truth was dawning in her mind.

"It isn't the sofa," said Ernestine.

Her mother took the package, and opened it. It contained a netted hood, coarse, but warm.

"Who is this for?"

"I bought it for Mary Allen."

"Her Christmas gift?"

"Yes."

"It was very kind, and very thoughtful in you, dear," said the mother, speaking calmly, though with an effort. And she stooped down and kissed the lips of her child. "God bless you!" was spoken in her heart, though the benediction came not forth into words.

"Who is Mary Allen?" asked the father.

"The child of a poor woman who has done some plain sewing for me. She needs a warm hood, and Ernestine's Christmas gift will be a timely one, I am sure."

What a loving look was cast by the father upon his child. How his heart stirred within him.

"I wonder if Mary Allen doesn't need a pair of warm stockings, and stout shoes as well?" he said, looking down into the face of Ernestine.

"Oh, yes, Father; I know she does!" The child spoke eagerly, and with a hopeful expression in her eyes.

"You shall add them to your gift, to-morrow," said the father.

"I shall be so happy!" And Ernestine clapped her little hands together in the fervor of her delight.

"It is more blessed to give than to receive." The mother's voice, full of meaning for the ears of Ernestine, trembled as she uttered these words, which were radiant with light. But the child felt their meaning still deeper, as she stood at her window on the next day, which was Christmas — a day of icy coldness — and saw Mary Allen go past, wearing a comfortable hood in place of the old, thin bonnet, and having warm stockings, and new shoes upon her feet. Ernestine received many beautiful gifts on that day, and she was very happy; but her joy in giving was deeper, purer, and more abiding, than her joy in receiving.

XVI.

THE HELPING HAND.

"NOT even a word of recognition!" The speaker was a woman. Over her gentle face had fallen a shadow of disappointment. She was sitting at a table, in a plainly furnished room, with books, magazines, and writing materials before her. In her hand was a literary review, the last page of which she had just turned.

"Not even a word of recognition!" she repeated, in a tone of discouragement. "Every book but mine noticed; mine, into which my heart went with such a loving interest. I am hurt, and can not help it!"

She laid her cheek upon her hand, and sat, soberfaced, for a long time. Then arousing, with a sigh, she turned to the table, and shutting her portfolio, murmured,

"Yes, it may be so. Only a few possess distinguishing literary ability; only a few have power to command the public attention and move the public heart. I am not, it seems, of the number. Ah, well! It is of no use striving with the inevitable. I must step aside, and give place to men and women of higher endowments."

She arose, and began walking, with slow, even steps, the floor of her room. After a while she resumed her place at the writing table. She had just seated herself when a servant came in and handed her two magazines and a letter. She glanced at the letter, and not recognizing it as from any known correspondent, deferred breaking the seal until she had looked into the magazines, which ought to contain notices of her book. Her hand was nervous as she cut the leaves of the first one opened; and her eyes went, hurriedly, from page to page. Then she became motionless and intent. There was recognition here! Twice she read the notice of her book; then leaned back in her chair, with wet lashes quivering on her crimson cheeks.

"Feeble, commonplace, and harmless. We may commend the volume to parents as a safe one to introduce among children."

That was the recognition.

"Feeble and commonplace." The tears which had wet her lashes swelled now to a flood and ran over her cheeks. She was hurt to the quick. Earnestly, thoughtfully, and with true and delicate perceptions of mental and moral states, had she written, thinking more of the good to be done than of the fame to be acquired. She had intruded her consciousness, with a clear seeing vision, into the actual of human life, and held a mirror up to nature. But the critic, dipping in here and there, and scanning this page and that, out of all just connection, saw only commonplace things and trite moral sentiments. No brilliant passages arrested him; no gorgeous cloud-castles of thought which the sun of reason dissolves into airy nothings; no ambitious paradings of sounding and unusual words meant to conceal meagre thoughts; no, nothing of these were found: and so, without taking time to comprehend the author, her book was thrown aside with the easy utterance of "feeble, commonplace, and harmless," and thought of no more.

Nearly ten minutes went by, and then the other magazine was opened.

"Writes carelessly at times"—a little more attention to style would give greater acceptability to her works"—"nothing very brilliant or striking; but a deal of human nature and solid sense"—"will do good in her day, but scarcely be heard of in the next generation: books of this class do not live."

There were some flashings of indignant feeling from the no longer wet eyes; lips curled proudly and a little defiantly. Our author was but human. The simple love of doing good was not strong enough to bear her calmly through an experience like this.

"A lady wishes to see you," said the servant, opening the door again.

"Who is it?" was inquired.

The servant gave her a card, on which she read the name of a friend.

"Say that I will be down in a moment."

The servant withdrew, and she made a few trifling but hurried changes in her toilet.

"I fear my visit may be an intrusion on your time," said the friend, as they stood with warmly clasped hands; "but I felt constrained to call this morning."

"No visit from you can ever be an intrusion," was replied. Light was breaking through the face over which clouds lay a moment before.

"I have just finished your new book," went on the visitor. "As I turned the last page I felt a strong desire to tell you how much good it had done me. My mind was in darkness as to a great principle of life when I commenced reading. This principle you illustrated in so clear a manner that I now see it as in noonday light. I thank you, my sister, for true words distinctly spoken

—thank you not only in my own name, but in the name of thousands to whom they will come in blessing. God has given you the power to move hearts, and, what is still better, the will to move them for good."

Dry eyes were wet again.

"There can be no higher praise than this!" was modestly answered. "Whatever power I possess is, as you have said, God's gift; and I pray ever that He will show me how best to use it in His work. I am not very strong of wing; I cannot, eagle-like, dwell above the mountains. At best I am a home-bird, singing under the eaves, or cooing at the windows."

"The birds we love and cherish," said the friend. "But why do I see tears on cheeks that should be radiant with smiles?"

"The heart is weak. It is not always satisfied with the simple doing of good. To do good is so easy, so unimposing, so unattractive, and commonplace. The world admires the brilliant and the aspiring; will stand gazing at the eagle as he rises toward the sun, all indifferent to the robin, the thrush, or the dove. The imposing and the difficult extort admiration, while a simple good deed is often misjudged as pharisaical, and earnest admonition to do right sneered at as cant."

"Dear friend, I can not bear this from you," answered the visitor. "Why in so strange a state? You are not envious of the eagle?"

" Oh, no, no! Not envious, I trust."

" What then?"

" I am human, and human nature is weak. We cannot, unmoved, hear our work depreciated."

" Has yours been depreciated?"

" Yes. This book, which has helped you, meets with no favor from critics. One passes it as of no account, not so much as announcing its publication, while another calls it dull and harmless. I should not care for this, I know. But the heart is weak. Such things hurt and discourage me. I feel as if I had no true power."

" And yet you have power to move the heart and enlighten the understanding, as thousands can testify. You need not care for a superficial or prejudiced critic, if you can speak to the people, and stir the common pulse. Your work is with and for the people. You comprehend their daily life-trials, and are gifted with ability to speak to them understandingly. Your work is not to amuse, nor to extort admiration, but to help. You do not write from a poor selfish desire to get praise and fame, but to do good — good in all degrees of life, from the highest to the lowest. And few, my friend, have been more successful. I would rather have your sheaves in my garner on that day when the Lord of the Harvest shall come, than the sheaves of any worker that I know in your field of labor. I say this sincerely, and may it give you comfort and strength! Don't, as Emmerson says, think, in your work, of its *acceptability*, but of its *excellence*. Do it always earnestly and well, according to the gifts by which you are endowed of God, and He will take care that no hand obstruct its course. Just so sure as it is vital with the power of helping your brother or your sister in weakness, or of lighting them in a dark way, will He make your voice heard."

"I thank you for such strong words of encouragement," said our desponding one, as the calm dignity of conscious strength and purity of motive came back into her face; "and thank you, especially, for that last suggestion. Emerson has struck the right key — has given the true philosophy. I have been thinking more of the acceptability of my work than of its excellence; more of what might be *said of it* than of what it *was*. Thanks, again, for this helping hand in a moment of weakness! I shall be stronger, I trust, in the future."

Alone, after this friend had departed, and stronger than before she came, the criticism that stung so sharply was read again.

"'Writes carelessly at times.' That is a fault," she said, "and should be corrected. 'A little more attention to style would give greater acceptability to her works.' Then it is my duty to give it more attention;

and I will endeavor, and feel obliged and not hurt by the suggestion. 'Nothing very brilliant or striking, but a deal of human nature and solid sense.' Why, that is a positive compliment! I read it as a sneer before; but now it has a tone of sincerity and good-will. 'Will do good in her day, but scarcely be heard of in the next generation; books of this class do not live.'"

The closing sentence touched the quick again. Not heard of in the next generation! No permanent life in such books! It was hard to accept of that judgment.

"But what," she asked herself, as right thoughts took their right position in her mind, "have I to do with the next generation? My work is in the present, and if I can do good in my day, the effect will not only go to the next generation, but to all generations. As to the life of my work, if there be in it a heavenly vitality it will not soon die."

The letter which had accompanied the magazines, and which had been forgotten, now looked up from the table and claimed attention. The seal was broken:

"DEAR LADY,— Forgive this freedom; but my heart is so full of thankfulness that I am constrained to write. Your last book has been to me a saviour and a consoler. Oh, in what a midnight of passion and error was my soul groping, when light came to me through you, and I saw a gulf at my feet! Back, back, back I moved, shuddering! And now I am on firm ground, with reason clear and conscience in her place. How clearly, yet how tenderly and lovingly, did you demonstrate a truth, which, had it come to me in almost any other way, I would have rejected. But as a gentle, wise, and considerate sister you approached me, and laying your hand on my arm, said 'Come and let us reason together.' You first won my confidence, then beguiled my interest, and then told me the truth in such calm, direct, and earnest words that I was convinced, warned, and saved. God bless you, my sister! You will never know the good you are doing until it is revealed in the world to come. Go on — go on, in Heaven's name! The heart of a stranger blesses you, and says, faint not, fail not."

Tears flooded the lady's face again; but there was no bitterness in them now. The helper was helped in her hour of weakness, and strengthened against the enemies of her peace — enemies, we mean, who were lurking in her own bosom, and exciting pride, ambition, and love of fame, so that they might act as hindrances. Stronger, calmer, and in a nobler spirit even than before, she turned to her work again, and gave to it that living vitality by which it had power to overcome evil and establish good. Neglect and cold unappreciative criticism had made her comprehend her own weakness, and been the means of opening her mind more interiorly, so that it could receive a higher influx of light. She was stronger and wiser from self-conquest, and thence able to infuse more of wisdom and human love in all that came from her hand.

XVII.

COMING DOWN.

THE "Country Parson," in one of his essays, has brought into view the difference between "giving up" and "coming down," an essay which may be specially commended to a class of over-ambitious people, who aiming too high, lose heart by failure, and give up all aspiring efforts, instead of gracefully coming down to the level of their ability, and on that plane doing earnest work in the world.

A case in point is that of a friend. He was, when quite a young man, overweeningly ambitious. As a boy at school, he sought to be first among his companions — head in the class, and leader in the play ground. But as his range of intellect fell below that of certain other boys, who, if not ambitious to stand higher than the rest, still towered above them by virtue of natural growth, he was continually in the experience of humiliations, and full of jealousies. It was a common thing for him to retire from the playground, because another boy was selected to a post of honor which he desired to fill, thus giving up and sulking, instead of coming down to the place assigned him by general consent, and filling it for his own pleasure and the gratification of his schoolmates. It was also a common thing for him to lose temper, pout, and grow sullen, if rivalled in an advance position in the class through superior scholarship in another boy. From this cause he gave much annoyance to the teachers, and involved himself in unpleasant discipline, and often in severe punishments.

Such was my friend at school. In selecting a pursuit in life, this weakness of character came in as a determining element. He must, in some way, stand out from, and above the common mass. He must be distinguished in the eyes of his fellows. His father, a careful, plodding man of trade, who had always managed to lay up something every year, was desirous that his son should, on leaving school, enter his store, and qualify himself to take part in a well established and sure business, that would ultimately fall entirely into his hands, but Asa Grant — that was my friend's name —

shrunk back from such an absorption of himself into the undistinguishable mass of common men. His was a higher ambition.

There was trouble at home about this choice of occupation. Old Mr. Grant was a plain, blunt man of the world, of limited education, but shrewd. He looked straight through pretension, and read the characters of most men as easily as he could read the pages of a book. Of his son's calibre he knew sufficient to be well convinced that, as a professional man, he could never rise above respectable mediocrity ; and the worldly, or rather, money-advantages appertaining to that position in law, medicine or theology, were so much below what he could promise his son in a prosecution of the business he had founded, that he was insensible to all arguments on the side against which he had arrayed himself.

But Mrs. Grant, the mother of Asa, who in marrying, had gone down a little — so thought her family of proud good-for-nothings, and so felt she — was entirely on her son's side. She was an ambitious mother, and encouraged her boy in his aspirations. Law and medicine were both discussed. Slow and toilsome ways to distinction. Asa looked along the dreary vista that opened in advance of him, as he soberly debated a choice between these two professions, and at times his heart would fail. No wonder that he hesitated. There was no royal road to eminence for him. He must win the goal, if at all, like an Olympian racer, through strength and speed.

My friend did not lack conceit. He rated his intellectual powers at a high average. No modest doubts were likely to hold him back from a contest in any arena. His decision was bending in favor of law, influenced by certain triumphs in a debating club, because, as a lawyer, he would get more distinctly in range of the public eye than as a physician, when an event occurred that changed the whole direction of his thoughts. This event was a " revival " in the church to which his parents belonged. Drawn into the sphere of this, and making, in consequence, certain new acquaintances among clergymen and young men piously inclined, the leading impulses of his mind opened the way for a new influx of ideas. The pulpit was to become his arena.

So my friend elected to study for the ministry. After sundry contests with his father on the subject, in which his mother was uniformly on his side, the old gentleman yielded a reluctant consent, and Asa went for a couple of years to a theological seminary. Here our ways separated, and we met, afterwards, only at unfrequent interval, though, by letter, we often held communication. Notwithstanding the weak side of Grant's character, he had many good qualities, and I was sincerely attached to him. After leaving college, he was invited to fill a pulpit in a small town of New Jersey. In a letter received from him at this time, and while debating whether to accept or decline the invitation, he said: "I can't think of burying myself in a little country village, among boorish and illiterate people. I have talents and aspirations for something better." My answer to this sentence was: "The work that comes to your hand, do with all your might. If I understand it, the souls of boorish and illiterate people, as you call them, are quite as precious in God's eyes as the souls of the most refined and educated. Bear in mind, my friend, that you have entered upon His work, and do not hesitate about going to any part of the field His providence may indicate." He replied from the parish which had given him his first call, informing me that he had concluded to accept, and giving as his chief reason the pulpit practice he would gain.

He remained two years in this place, seeking, during the time, all available opportunities to exchange with other ministers, in order to get before as many congregations as possible, and thus acquire something beyond a local reputation. He also wrote for the various periodicals of his church, generally signing his name to his articles, or in some way indicating their authorship. I often received copies of these articles, marked for my special attention. They were tolerably well written, but only from the memory. I could rarely find a trace of original thought. At the end of two years, and after the event of preaching three unsuccessful trial sermons before a New York congregation that was seeking for a minister, my friend resigned his pulpit, and came home to his father's to recreate, and also to work for a call from some better parish than the one under the bushel of which he had been hiding his light. Rather than "come down" to the level of humbler duties that fitted his tastes, he was willing to " give up," at least for a while.

A year of unsatisfying idleness was followed by the acceptance of another call from a country parish. "I am going to bury myself again." So he wrote on leaving for his new home. This sentence tells the story of his state. Here he preached, and wrote for the church periodicals, and aspired to a more notable position for two or three years, when a party in the congregation, that saw through him, became strong enough to induce a resignation. Half disgusted with his profession, my friend went home, and spent another period of fretful inaction. What particularly galled him was the fact that ministers, far his inferior in every way, according as he estimated them — were selected for the most desirable places, while he, to use his own language, was "left out in the cold."

Ten years afterwards I met my friend again. During this interval of time I had nearly lost sight of him, our paths in life having taken a strong divergence. Stepping from a railroad car at a watering station, near a village in central New York, I met Grant on the platform. The meeting was one of genuine pleasure on both sides. I had only left the car in order to stretch my limbs and get a few drafts of pure air, while the engineer supplied himself with water; but my friend insisted that I should give him a day or two, for the sake of "auld lang syne," and as my journey was for health, not business, I yielded on short debate. A drive of half an hour, through pleasant country lanes, in my friend's carriage, brought me to a snug cottage, just outside of a thrifty looking village, into which I was ushered, and presented to Mrs. Grant, whom I had never seen before. My friend had been married seven years. His wife impressed me, at the first glance, as a woman of character and cultivation. Her eyes were large and serious, and rested on my face, as she offered her hand, with a look of searching inquiry. I noticed this peculiarity — the look of inquiry, almost suspicious — and it gave me a feeling of discomfort. It was so much taken from the cordial welcome of my friend. Apart from this, my impression of Mrs. Grant was favorable, and I was soon aware that she was a woman of more than common intelligence.

It was late in the afternoon when I arrived. Tea was served early, and after tea we went to my friend's study, his wife, who had become interested in our conversation, accompanying us. It was natural that I should inquire as to my friend's life and prospects. This was a subject nearest his heart, as quickly appeared.

"I am simply buried in this place," was his response, in a dissatisfied voice.

I noticed a movement in his wife, and glancing towards her, saw that she was looking regretfully, almost sadly, at her husband.

"How large is your congregation?" I asked.

"Not above three hundred average attendance," he replied, in a depreciating tone. "A congregation of three hundred poorly educated people, in an out-of-the-way country town, is a settlement, after some twelve or fourteen years in the ministry, wholly outside of my poorest anticipations. I looked for something higher, as you well know. For a wider sphere — an arena worthy of myself."

I noticed a shadow falling over his wife's face as he thus talked. Not venturing a response, my friend continued:

"I am about discouraged. Men of half my ability — pardon this seeming egotism; but every man knows, or ought to know, the range of his capacity as compared with that of others — are preferred before me, and selected by city congregations that I could serve with double their effectiveness. There is something wrong in all this; management and underhand work, I must conclude. Forgive my reference to an unpleasant subject, but I am feeling sore just now. A parish in Albany was vacant, and I was invited to spend a few weeks there and preach, in order that the people might have an opportunity of seeing and hearing me. I went as desired, and preached four times. I never had a more attentive and sympathetic audience — never was more in freedom — never liked a people in their social relations, as far as I came in contact with them, half so well as I liked the people of that parish. I could understand them, and they could understand me. Two months have passed since my visit, and during all that time I daily looked for a call. Imagine my disappointment — my chagrin — on opening our church paper yesterday, to find announced the call to this very congregation of a third-rate man, brother to one of the most influential members. I am disgusted at all this! It doesn't suit me. The right man should be in the right place. He is not in the right place, and I am not in mine. After thirteen years of unappreciated and nearly fruitless labor in the ministry, I have about reached the conclusion that it is time to abandon the field."

I saw the shadow falling more heavily over his wife's face; saw moisture gathering in her large eyes, that were dwelling upon him.

"Three hundred souls," I remarked, in the silence that followed his concluding sentence, speaking deliberately, and with an impressiveness of manner that corresponded with my feelings, "are precious fruits, if you can garner them in the harvest time."

A light flashed over Mrs. Grant's countenance, and she gave me a single grateful look, that was a revelation of her state; then rising, at the call of a child, she left the study. Her husband regarded me in evident surprise, and some perplexity of thought. He had not anticipated such a response.

"Three hundred souls, committed to your care by God, make your position one of high responsibility," I resumed, as his wife closed the door, and we were alone. "Shall I speak out freely of what is now in my thought? or will you regard the plain speech of an old friend as intrusive?"

"Hold nothing back. I know your heart." There was a low thrill in his voice, as if from the presence of sudden pain, or dread. Evidently, my language had formed the basis in his mind of some startling convictions.

"I see that time and experience have not changed you in one particular," I said.

"What?"

"As a young man you were ambitious."

"I was, and I am."

"Ambitious for what?"

"To excel," he replied. "To be first in whatever I undertake."

"For the sake of excellence or use?" I queried.

"For the sake of use, I hope." But his voice dropped from its tone of confidence.

I did not resume immediately, that he might have time to look inward, in self-examination.

"Let me suggest a query," I said, after a brief silence.

"Say on." He shrunk a little in his arm-chair, as if bracing himself for a painful thrust.

"Perhaps we had better change the subject, and talk pleasantly of old times."

"No — no," he replied, firmly. "Say on. You have opened a window in my thoughts, through which a few rays of light are streaming. Perhaps you can give me more light. At any rate, I wish to hear."

I then said:

"Has it never occurred to you, that an humbler estimate of your abilities than the one you have maintained, might be nearer the truth? That, in fact, you have always soared, in thought, too high; and that, to be really useful, according to the range of your ability, you must come down to your work in a lower sphere?"

It was painful to see the effect of this, striking as it did at his very self-hood — at the very life-impulses of his whole character. His face grew very pale; his lips fell slowly apart; his eyes rounded into an almost frightened stare.

"It will not do," I continued, "for God's minister to act over his school-boy weaknesses; to refuse to spell because another has got above him in the class — to give up because he must go down."

He covered his face with his hands, that he might conceal from me the emotions he could not repress. I saw that a low quiver was running through his frame.

"God forbid that I should say this, my friend, to hurt! I speak from my high regard — from my yearning wish to serve. I meet you, in a great crisis of your life, at a point where two ways open before you, and I am concerned that you take the right way. I find you with three hundred souls in charge, yet complaining that you have not scope and verge enough. The Lord of the vineyard may possibly know best; and I think you will be happier if you diligently work the field where He has placed you; if you come down to a sphere lower than your ambition has desired, and, doing your duty, leave all the rest to Him.

For the space of several minutes he sat with his face still hidden. I was in doubt whether I had helped or offended him. But I had gone as far as I thought prudent, and so awaited his response. It came. Withdrawing his hands from his face, that was still pale, but now wearing a subdued aspect, he said:

"What a revelation of myself you have given! In all these dissatisfied, unprofitable years, I have been striving for a position; seeking for the praise of men; contending for honors — instead of bringing my life down into my work with the sole end of doing good. You have hurt me in a tender place — you have revealed my nakedness — but you are the truest friend of my life, and even in this moment of bitter suffering I offer thanks. Three hundred souls to care for; three hundred souls to lead heavenward — and yet impatient for a wider sphere! If not faithful with three hundred, shall I be trusted with thousands?"

The study door opened quietly, and his wife came in. My friend ceased speaking.

"Am I intruding?" Mrs. Grant paused a few steps from the door.

"Not at all," was my answer, rising to make room for her.

But her eyes were on her husband's countenance. She saw in it a great change. It was for him to say whether her presence were acceptable or not.

"Sit down, Margaret." He spoke kindly, yet very soberly. I noticed that her face was full of eager questionings, and that she looked on him with a most tender yet anxious concern.

"I shall not leave here, Margaret." I saw her countenance lighten.

"I shall not abandon my work because it lies out of the sphere of general observation, and does not reward me with the praises of men. God helping me, I will come down to it in a spirit of self-denial and self-devotion, justly accordant with the office I have assumed."

It was as if a gleam of sunshine had been flung across the face of Mrs. Grant. I saw her eyes glisten.

"Go up to it, rather," I said, "on the stairway of spiritual ascent — up, interiorly, to higher planes of life and usefulness. The coming down of which you speak is only a descent on the external and worldly side, in order that you may rise on the inner and spiritual side to mountain hights that reach upward into heaven."

Mrs. Grant turned and looked at me while I spoke with a glad and grateful expression. I noticed that she had little to say, and that when she did speak her words were guarded, lest her husband's sensitive pride should in any way be hurt, and thus obscurity of mind follow. She saw the true way opening before him, and trembled in fear of some obstruction that might turn him aside ere sufficient progress were made to show him the better country through which he was journeying.

As we sat at breakfast on the next morning, I spoke of leaving in the afternoon. My friend would not hear to it; and his wife, who had received me with almost a suspicous scrutiny, joined warmly in her husband's plea, that I would remain at least another day.

"Not yet," she said, on the following afternoon, as I sat alone with her, and, in a pause of the conversation, referred to the succeeding day as that of my departure. "Remain a little longer with us. You are the truest friend my husband has known, for you have helped him to an understanding of himself. The thought of his giving up because dissatisfied with the sphere of labor in which God's providence has placed him, instead of coming right down with earnestness into his work, pained me beyond expression. I could not help him with my woman's reasonings; and my perceptions did not penetrate his thoughts. He could not see as I saw, nor feel as I felt; and I knew that he was drifting away from safe anchorage. God sent you in the right time, and put right words in your mouth. Stay yet a little longer, and speak other words, each of which shall be as a nail in a sure place."

My visit was prolonged for nearly a week. On leaving my friend he said, as he held my hand with a tight grip:

I will be no longer as a school-boy, pouting and giving up because I cannot be head; but a man, doing the best I can wherever I am."

"And thus," I answered, "you will grow wiser, better, and stronger every day, and, like water, find by an unfailing law, the level of your ability."

In the years that followed my friend went up to a higher place, both externally and internally. A weak ambition had hindered a just development of his powers. But in coming down to the work in hand, and entering into it with a patient effort to do it well, he naturally grew wiser and stronger, and, in due time, was called to richer and broader fields where he now labors. In "going down" he had not "given up," and here lay the secret of his right development.

XVIII.

THE POET'S LESSON.

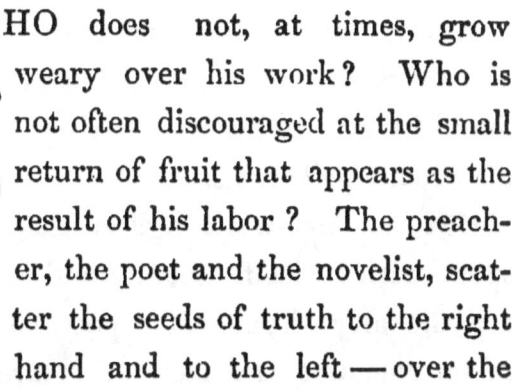WHO does not, at times, grow weary over his work? Who is not often discouraged at the small return of fruit that appears as the result of his labor? The preacher, the poet and the novelist, scatter the seeds of truth to the right hand and to the left — over the plowed field and by the barren wayside — and then go on their ways. The seed may strike its living roots into the inviting soil, and send up green blades to flutter in the sunshine; and there may come sweet blossoms, with fruits and grain — yet, the preacher and the poet may never hear of the golden harvests that crowned their labor with blessings. They would be more than human, were they not often discouraged; did not often faint by the way; sighed not, often, for a wider and clearer responce.

So it was with Adrian, the poet and teacher of life-lessons, whose voice found echoes in thousands and thousands of hearts all over the length and breadth of the land. So it was, with him, as he sat alone on New Year's Eve, listening now to the shrill whistle of the blast without, and now to its sobbings and moanings, as it lingered along the shaggy eaves, and among the gables and towering chimneys.

Adrian was sadder than usual on this wintry New Year's Eve. The hand of some unkindly spirit had found its way to his heart strings and swept them with discordant pulsations.

"Is not my work lighter than vanity?" Thus he spoke with himself, moodily and despondingly. "What are the airy rhymes of a poet, or the light tissues of fable, romance and story, that are woven by his pen? Does not the wind bear them up and away as if they were gossamer? A blast of the angry tempest, and where are they? The statesman wields a nation's destiny. He sets his mark upon the age, and history points back to him through a thousand generations. The merchant brings together the very ends of the earth, and unites empires by bonds of mutual benefits. Look at the engineer, the builder, the sublime astronomer, the noble historian! Alas! Am I not the weakest, the poorest, the meanest in the world? Let me die, and make no sign."

Unhappy Adrian! What false spirit hast thou admitted into the guest-chamber of reason? It has not always been so with thee. Not many days have passed since a deep and pure delight was given thee in thy work — a delight passing the comprehension of many.

The evening waned, and Adrian, having wearied himself with unhappy thoughts and feelings, sunk quietly away into sleep. Blessed sleep! How opportunely it comes, with its veil of oblivion. Blessed sleep! Is there a dweller upon the earth who has not uttered these words in fervent thankfulness many, many times? Sleep changes the progressive order of our lives. Volition ceases, and with volition the fret and fever of existence. As the action of all voluntary muscle in the body ceases, so ceases the action of all the voluntary faculties of the mind. Come we then, of course, more directly under heavenly guardianship, and heavenly influence. How sweetly is the spirit tranquilized! No matter how violently may have raged the storms of passion ere nature claimed her hours of sleep, the morning surely comes to us in calmness and peace.

Adrian slept; and there came dreams to his sleep. One dream was after this wise:

He was walking across a barren field, along a narrow path that led him at last to the door of a poor laborer's cottage. It was near the close of day. In the door of the cottage sat a woman, and two children stood by her, listening attentively while she read. They did not appear to notice Adrian, though he drew so close to them that he could hear every word that fell from the woman's lips. Suddenly his heart leaped with a strange delight. The words to which she was giving voice were his own words. He had written them many years before, earnestly desiring that they might find their way into children's hearts, and bear with them a blessing.

The mother read on, and the children leaned towards her. Adrain saw that the pure lessons he had given were sinking into their young minds.

"I will be like that good man," said one of the children, as his mother ceased reading.

"And I will try to be like the sweet young lady, his daughter," said the other.

"Such good examples, my children, are for our imitation," answered the mother. "We are poor, but we may all have the riches about which we are told in the story — riches of love and wisdom from our Father in Heaven. Possessing these, we can do much good to others as we pass through life; and to do good, my children, is to be happy."

Like one of those dissolving views that charm while they delude the senses, changed this humble scene into one of external grace and beauty. Adrian was in the luxurious apartment of a lady grown life-weary through idleness. She lay, half reclined, on a sofa, her countenance wearing a fretful aspect. As before, his presence seemed not observed. Sighs parted her lips — sad words were uttered — her restless body was constantly changing its positions.

"Oh, I am wretched!" she murmured. "Existence is a tiresome burden. It were better to die and be at rest, than live this aimless, miserable life."

Even while she spoke, a beautiful young maiden came gliding into the room. She held an open book in her hand. With a winning smile, she said —

"Oh, Aunt, I have found something that you will be charmed to hear. Let me read it to you."

"No, child" — and the lady put up her hands. "I am in no mood for reading."

But the sweet girl would take no denial. Drawing an ottoman to the lady's feet, she sat down and read. How familiar was the language which fell from her lips! Adrian listened. It was a simple allegory that the maiden read; yet the truth it illustrated could not fail, if it reached any mind, to awaken aspirations towards goodness. And he had composed that allegory years gone by — composed, and sent it forth on its mission.

At first, the lady was restless; and it was plain that she repressed her impatience only by an effort. But all at once she became quiet, and leaned her head in a listening attitude; nor did she move until the reading was over — then the whole aspect of her face was changed. It was no longer depressed, nor fretful, but had about it a calmness and elevation that was pleasant to look upon.

"I knew that it would stir your soul with better feelings, Aunt," said the maiden.

"And it has done so," was the earnestly spoken reply. "If I could only rest in the teachings of that charming little story — could only, as the sweet lady therein described, forget myself in loving others — life would put on a new charm. Thanks to the author for his lesson of wisdom! Do you know his name, my child?"

Adrian held his breath. He knew that his own name would come in music from the maiden's lips, and it did come, sending through every fibre of his spirit a thrill of exquisite pleasure.

"May God bless him for the good he has done!" said the lady, warmly. "And may God help me to profit well by the lesson I have now received."

"Will you go with me to-day on a visit to old Mrs. Armour?" asked the maiden, pressing to immediate action the good impulses that were stirring in the heart of the lady.

"To-day?" There was an air of reluctance about the speaker.

"Yes, to-day, Aunt. Remember the lady in the story, and her motto — 'Let no good impulse wait until to-morrow.' Mrs. Armour will be so glad to see you."

Thus urged the lady consented. And so the story of Adrain brought a double blessing, and he had *his* reward.

Faded this scene like the other; and now a low wail of grief penetrated his ears. Looking up, he saw a woman heavily draped in the garments of mourning. She sat by a table on which lay some books. In her hand she held the miniature of her child; and Adrian knew that it was her child, and that it had passed upwards to dwell with angels. Tears blinded the grieving mother's eyes, as she tried to look upon the pictured face of her departed. Friend after friend came into the room, and sought to comfort the mourner; but she turned from them, and wept on. Their words had in them no touch of healing. And so they left her alone in her sorrow. All grief spends itself, sobbing away into silence, like the departing tempest. The lady grew calm at length; and thought began to reach out from the darkness wherein it was shrouded, to find something upon which it could rest and gain support in this hour of bitter trial. Now her hand moved upon the books that lay upon the table; now it rested upon a volume in blue and gold;

and now a page was opened before her, and her eyes fell upon words that instantly fixed her attention. The book was one of Adrian's — he knew it at a glance.

The lady read, and a gradual change was soon apparent. The almost hopeless anguish of her countenance softened away into resignation — and her eyes, so stony in their expression a little while before, were growing tender, meek, and patient. Closing the book, at length, she lifted her gaze upwards and said, in a subdued voice —

"Father, I thank thee for these words of comfort and hope, that must have been written for me. Upon the darkness of my sorrow light has broken. A veil has been drawn aside, and I see that in love thou hast visited me — for only in love are thy dealings with the children of men. By thy inspiration has the poet spoken; and I take his words as messages from thee. Thy hand is near me in this grief, and thy arm is extended to support me. Light has come through the heavily curtained windows, and I see thy Providence as in noonday light."

There was a pause. The lady's eyes fell to the book, and she read on again.

"Thanks, Poet and Comforter! Thy mission is high and noble," she said, closing the book at length. "May Heaven's choicest blessings be showered upon thy heart."

And this scene changed also. Adrian was now in the street, moving along with the promiscuous crowd. Two young men went by him. They were in conversation. Something impelled him to follow; and, as he did so, he heard all that passed between them. One, the youngest, seemed bent on doing something, from the consummation of which his older companion was trying to dissuade him. But, though he urged many strong considerations, the boy — for he was only a boy, in fact — swerved not a hair from his purpose.

"Leave me," he said, with all the firmness he could assume. "Leave me, I say!"

"No, Edward, my friend, I cannot leave you," answered the elder companion. "You are wrong to put yourself in the way of temptation."

"Don't fear for me. I know myself," was returned, with considerable impatience of manner.

"I do fear for you. You do not know yourself nor the almost irresistible influence which a number of persons, all consenting to a single act, have over individuals who come within their sphere."

"It is in vain; and now good night. Let us part here. I will see you to-morrow morning. Goodnight!"

And the determined boy sought to escape from his friend; but the friend loved him too truly to suffer him to go, alone, into paths where a false step might prove his ruin. Laying hold upon his arm, he said, in a tone full of interest and persuasion —

"Edward, let me repeat to you something which I read in a book to-day. It arrested my attention at the time, and now comes up in my thoughts with singular vividness."

"To-morrow, I will hear it," said the young man, petulantly.

"No, you must hear it to-night — Listen!"

And then Adrian heard this faithful friend repeat, with singular truth to style and language, a little composed life-history, which years before he had written and cast forth upon human minds as bread is cast upon the waters. In writing this life-history, he had come into a most vivid perception of the power of evil enticements over minds of a certain temperament, and had, with a wonderful truth to nature, drawn character, incident, action, and consequence, in their relation and progression. So startling and life-like were the scenes presented, and so painful the final result, that, when the last sentence fell from the monitor's lips, his young friend turned on him a pallid face. There was a pause, and silence, for some moments.

"Come!" said the friend, gently.

"Saved! Saved!" Almost sobbed the now subdued, repentant boy, as he grasped the arm of his companion.

Adrian awoke! The wintry wind still moaned and wailed without, but it had no power to sadden the poet's heart; for he heard music in its tones. This dream was to him a revelation of the truth. He knew that in his work were good seeds; and now he felt assured that if good seeds were scattered upon human hearts, some of them must fall upon good ground, and bring forth fruit in the harvest time.

"To inspire the heart with noble and virtuous impulses; to send rays of comfort into souls darkened by sorrow; to help the weak; give sight to the blind wanderer in the mazes of error, and to hold back the steps from sin — are not these great deeds?"

And Adrian's heart began to swell with joy as he talked thus with himself; for a deeper insight had been given, and a clearer perception of truth vouchsafed.

Poet, novelist, preacher! The lesson is yours. Weary not over your tasks; faint not under your burdens; permit no shadows from the wing of doubt to dim the clear eye of faith. But work on in your high calling, sending abroad on every passing breeze the winged germs that shall fall upon good ground in thronged cities, distant hamlets, and solitary homes. Be diligent and faithful, and the Lord of the harvest will make your words fruitful. They shall go forth in light, in comfort, in strength, in blessing; and thousands upon thousands will thank God that you have lived and spoken. You will never know a hundredth part of the good you have done; but all will be written in the records of eternity.

XIX.

UP HIGHER.

"Down again!" I heard remarked, in a half pitying, half complaining way.

"Martin?"

"Yes; he's tripped again."

"So I heard this morning."

"Tripped, and gone down with a heavy fall; so heavy that I doubt if he recover himself again."

"I'm sorry for Martin," said the other. "He has always impressed me as a well-meaning man."

"Yes, well-meaning enough; but something more than well-meaning is required for success in this world."

"A spice of cunning and shrewdness, not to speak of roguery."

"Shrewdness is required, and forethought, and a number of other qualities not possessed, I think, in a high degree by Martin. As to the cunning and roguery, they may succeed for a time, but they always outwit themselves in the end."

"Poor fellow! Be the cause what it may, I pity him. He's tried hard enough to keep up. No man could have been more faithful to business, so far as the devotion of his time and his active attention were concerned. He deserved a better fate.'

"How will his affairs settle?"

"Not particularly well, I hear."

"Does he show a fair hand?"

"Oh yes." The answer was without hesitation.

"I might have known that from what I know of the man."

"I don't believe Martin would hold any thing back. He has always impressed me as a man who would pay to the uttermost farthing. Poor fellow! I'm sorry the fortunes of war are against him, and that he has gone down in the heat of battle, unvictorious."

"Yes, gone down, gone down, unvictorious," was responded, in a tone of pity.

It was the first intimation I had of Martin's failure in business, and I was pained to hear of his misfortune. I knew him very well, and held him, as a friend, in high personal regard. The testimony which had been borne in favor of his integrity was in agreement with my own estimate of his character.

Intelligence of this failure soon spread through all the business circles in which Martin was known, and for two or three days almost every other person you met had something to say about it. The ordinary way of referring to the subject was in the words, " Poor Martin, I hear, has gone down again." And not a few responded, " He's reached the bottom of the hill this time." Some pitied; some blamed; and some spoke harshly and angrily — the latter were of those who had lost by the failure. I felt grieved for Martin. It was a sad ordeal for a man of right feelings to pass through.

I did not meet him, except casually in the street, for some time after his failure. But passing his store one day, and seeing it closed, as a sign that he had given up business, I felt that, as one who had known him with some personal intimacy, I should not hold myself aloof in this his day of trouble. So I called at his house one evening. When I grasped his hand and looked into his face, I saw that he had not come through this trial without great suffering. He had the appearance of a man who had come recently from a bed of sickness.

"How are you, my friend?" I asked, as we sat down together.

"As well as could be hoped for," he replied, a feeble smile touching his lips with a ray of light.

"Cast down, but not forsaken."

"Not forsaken, I trust," he answered, in a firmer voice.

"This is one of the troubles that is hard to bear," said I.

"Yes; but, as in all other troubles, our strength is as our day."

"I am pleased to hear you say that," I remarked.

"I should be sorry, indeed, if I could not say it," he answered, still gaining steadiness of manner. "We look forward to great trials with a shuddering sense of fear, because we are conscious only of the feeble power of endurance that may be called our own. But when the trial comes, and we go down amidst the rushing waters, in fear and shuddering lest they overwhelm us, we find an arm to lean upon that is unseen but full of strength."

"And so your strength has been as your day?" said I.

"Yes; or I should have perished among the floods. That I sit here, and talk with you as a man to his friend, clothed and in my right mind, makes the fact evident."

"Could you not have prevented this disaster?" I asked, during our conversation.

"Yes," he replied, with such confidence in his voice that I said, with some earnestness,

"Then why did you not use the means?"

"Simply because I could not satisfy myself that they

were the right means. You shall hear and judge for yourself.

"Two months ago one of my customers, to whom I had sold rather more freely than my judgment afterwards approved, failed. It was only a few days before the notes which I had received in payment came due. These notes had been discounted, and I had, of course, to take care of them. In doing this the means held in reserve for maturing payments were exhausted for the time, and I was thrown upon the street as a borrower, on most disadvantageous terms. Another loss, following quickly on this one, alarmed and bewildered me. Twice before had I failed in business, and now this dreaded ordeal, more painful than death in my imagination, looked me in the face again, and I grew faint with heart-sickness. I looked eagerly this way and that. Caught at one expedient and another; dropping each in turn as of little promise, or as indefensible on the score of honest dealing.

"While sitting at my desk one day, searching about in my thought for a way of escape from the difficulties that environed me like a steadily approaching wall of fire, a real estate agent with whom I was well acquainted, came in, and said to me, in a confidential way,

"'I know where some money is to be gained, Mr. Martin.'

"'Money is a very desirable thing,' I answered.

"'And not always to be picked up in the street,' said he.

"'Not so far as my experience is concerned.'

"'Or mine either. Well, as I was saying,' he went on, 'I know where some money is to be made. Would you like to join me in making it?' I answered yes, without hesitation; for, of all things, money was what I then most wanted; and asked for a statement of the ways and means required.

"'In the first place,' said he, 'can you raise three or four thousand dollars within a week?'

"I said yes, if the amount was only needed temporarily; if for permanent investment, no.

"'It will only be needed temporarily,' he answered, 'as bait for taking a big fish.' And he smiled in a way that did not strike me as pleasant.

"'Explain yourself fully,' I now said, and he went on.

"'There is a piece of wild land in the interior of this State, which has been owned for years by two elderly maiden sisters, who, long ago, were sick of paying taxes on property that yielded no income. The tract includes nearly two thousand acres, and was bought originally at one dollar and a half an acre. It can be had to-day for three dollars an acre. I know the parties who own it, and they are now, as they have been for years, anxious to turn this property into money, which can be invested and insure an annual interest. They are advancing in life, and prefer a present certainty to large hopes in the future. I have known of the existence of this property for some time, and have had itching fingers toward it, because I felt satisfied from its location that it must contain valuable mineral desposits — coal or iron. Perhaps both. Last week I ran up into the region where it was situated, and getting a skilled man in the neighborhood, spent two days in a careful examination of the entire tract. The result more than confirmed my expectation. Coal crops out in many places, specimens of which I brought away. It proves, on testing, to be of superior quality. Moreover, a railroad is now in the course of construction, which will pass within three miles of the land. Why, Mr. Martin, this whole tract could be sold for a hundred thousand dollars in an hour, if its value was known in the market as I know it. Now, what I require to gain possession is the money. But unfortunately I am poor. I know twenty men who would clutch at the opportunity of joining me in the purchase, and put down the cash at a word; but I'm afraid to trust them with my secret. And this is why I come to you. If you can furnish the means required, one half of the land is yours. I have already seen the old ladies, and they are ready to sell the property for six thousand dollars ; one half cash, and the balance in six or twelve months' payments. The thing must be done quickly, or they may get an inkling of the truth. What do you say, Mr. Martin ? You can sell out your interest in a week for fifty thousand dollars !'

"Now this man was not a scheming visionary, who got rich on paper twenty times a year, but a cool, shrewd person, who understood entirely what he was about. If he had spent two days on the property referred to, in company with an expert, the report he made as to coal desposits might be fully relied upon. Here, then, was a way of escape made plain to me. I had but to raise the sum of three thousand dollars, which my credit would enable me to do, and hold my portion of this land until we could make its value known. I was on the point of thanking him for the offer of a share in so promising an enterprise, and saying that I would go in with him of course, when this question came into my mind : ' Is it right to take advantage of the ignorance of these old ladies, and get possession of their property at a mere tithe of its real worth ?' The question disturbed me considerably, and I endeavored to put it out of my mind. But it kept repeating itself, and growing more and more intrusive every moment.

"'What do you say?' asked the man, breaking in upon my long, hesitating silence.

"'In one hour I will give you an answer,' said I.

"This would afford me time to look at the subject on all sides. The temptation, under the dreadful pressure of my circumstances, was very great. In either of the previous ordeals through which I passed I would have yielded with scarcely a struggle. But I could not see, now, that a way of escape like this was defensible in any clear aspect of Christian morality. It was taking advantage of my better information to obtain valuable property for a most trifling consideration. Would this be in harmony with the Golden Rule? Would there be justice and judgment in the act? Was it a deed that any good conscience could bear onward to the closing of life, and not feel its pressure as a burden growing heavier and heavier? As I dwelt on the subject my mind grew excited and eager. On the one hand was inevitable ruin — my affairs were so near a crisis that hope had given way; on the other, a fortune as large as I had ever asked for lay within my reach, and I had only to put forth my hand and take it — only to put forth my hand and save myself from disaster and my creditors from loss. Then came the additional argument that my refusal to accept the advantage would not prevent the old ladies from losing this property. Some other person would be found to take my place in furnishing the cash required, and so the land would pass to new owners. But this did not satisfy me. It was the old false argument in favor of appropriating another's goods because they were doomed to be stolen by somebody.

"In an hour my tempter returned.

"'What's the word, Mr. Martin?' he asked, looking at me so confidently that I saw he was in no doubt about my acceptance of his proposal. I had settled the question, after a severe struggle, and was prepared to answer without hesitation.

"'The thing seems promising enough,' said I; 'but I have concluded against becoming a party in the transaction.'

"'Why not?' he asked, looking disappointed.

"'Plainly,' was my answer, 'because it hasn't a fair look. Advantage will be taken of another's ignorance.'

"The man's face betrayed an instant angry movement of his feelings, and he muttered something in an undertone, in which my ears seemed to detect the words, 'Stupid fool!'

"'And you are really in earnest?' said he, scarcely seeking to hide a look of contempt that was rising to his face.

"'I am,' was my firm answer.

"'Good-morning!'

"He threw the words at me with an impatient impulse, and left me on the instant."

"Did he find a less scrupulous individual to join him?" I asked.

"Yes; and what is more, the purchase of the land was made, and it has since been sold to a company for some fabulous sum — two or three hundred thousand dollars, I believe."

"Half of which would have been yours?" said I.

"Yes," he answered, without change of tone or manner.

"And instead of being away down in this low, dim valley, you would now be on the sunny heights of prosperity?"

He looked at me for a little while without answering.

"Have you, at any time, regretted that decision?" I asked.

"Not for a single instant," he replied. "After the temptation was over, and my mind was able to rise into a clearer region, I saw the transaction in such a hideous aspect that I almost shuddered in thinking of my escape. Ah! Sir, there are greater evils than poverty, and higher good than riches. With that sin upon my conscience I would have gone down into regions of doubt and darkness, and mayhap lost my way, never to find it again. It is better, far better, I think, to walk in the right way, even if it be with naked feet, than to tread on soft velvet in passing along the road that leads to destruction at last."

"Better? Yes, a thousand times better!" said I with ardor. "This fall, then — this 'going down' again, as the common saying is — can not, in one sense, be called a misfortune, but a trial in which there might come a death of something evil and selfish in your soul, and thence a new birth of higher and more heavenly principles. You were brought into a strong temptation, in which good gained a victory over evil; and you are a truer man for the fierce struggle and conquest."

"I know not how that may be," he answered. "I only know that I have a clear conscience; that in the fire through which I have been required to pass I have not let truth or justice go to the flames."

How think you, reader? Had that man gone down lower or up higher? What would you have done under circumstances of like trial? Would you have clutched eagerly at the golden opportunity which came with such tempting smiles; or, like Martin, risked the fire? If you are a man looking heavenward — and doubtless this is so — let the question come home; it may give you a new consciousness of your own state. In the mirror of his scrupulous action you may see a reflection of yourself.

XX.

WAS IT A MISFORTUNE.

"IMPOSSIBLE!" exclaimed Morris Heston, starting up from his desk. "Impossible!" he repeated, his face growing very pale.

"It is too true," was the answer made by a gentleman, who had come hurriedly into the store of Mr. Heston. "I have the news from a reliable source."

"Failed!"

"Yes; and failed badly. It is alleged that not ten cents in the dollar can possibly be realized. I hope he doesn't owe you much."

"Not a great deal," was answered, evasively, though with ill-concealed anxiety; "yet enough to sweep away nearly all my profits on the year's business, should the loss be total. Is he on your books?"

"Yes."

"To a large amount?"

"Three thousand dollars."

"I thought him sound to the core. The reports in regard to his standing have always been A No. 1."

"He has been engaged, it is said, in some land speculations, which have turned out disastrously. The old story of the dog and the shadow. Well, we must expect such things, and meet them with as much philosophy as can be summoned to our aid. Good morning."

And the man went out as hurriedly as he had come in. As he left the store, Mr. Heston turned, with a disturbed manner, to his ledger, and threw over the leaves nervously. Pausing at an account, he footed it up rapidly. The pencilled figures showed the sum of four thousand eight hundred and sixty-one dollars. There was a credit by bills receivable of four thousand dollars; three thousand five hundred of which had been discounted, and would mature in less than a month.

Morris Heston was a young man, who had been in business only about two years. The capital on which he commenced, was less than two thousand dollars; and the whole of this he had saved from his salary. He was active, industrious and intelligent, and on the road, many predicted, to fortune. But in one thing he was indiscreet; and that was, in selling too largely to a single customer. No wonder that he started and turned pale on hearing bad news from this customer; for loss here was equivalent to ruin. Already, the relation between receipts and payments were so close, that any serious deficiency in the one, or increase in the other, would prove a source of embarrassment; and to have between three and four thousand dollars of discounted bills come back upon him in four weeks, would certainly cause him to stop payment.

We need not picture the troubled events that followed, too surely, the confirmed intelligence of this failure of a distant customer. Heston was too weak to bear the pressure that came upon him, and so was forced to give way. A few of his creditors, who had faith in his integrity and ability, would cheerfully have reduced their claims, and given him ample time on the balance; but the majority, who had no personal interest in him, and looked only to themselves, acted upon the common adage current in such cases, that the "first loss is the best loss," and swept everything, leaving the unhappy, mortified and dispirited young man without a dollar on which to begin the world again — nay, even worse than this, leaving him several thousand dollars in debt; for, in throwing his stock into auction, and forcing collections, serious losses were inevitable.

Troubles rarely come alone. Another, and to our young friend, a sadder disaster followed. He was under engagement of marriage, and the time of its celebration had been fixed. From the moment rumor filled the air with reports of his heavy losses and danger of failure he thought he could perceive a change in the manner of his betrothed. He tried to think this only imagination; but the change seemed daily to grow more and more apparent. At last it became necessary for him to tell her of his misfortune, and the blight which had come over his worldly prospects. He still had faith in her; still tried to deceive himself notwithstanding the recent change in her manner.

She listened with a coldness of exterior that chilled him to the heart; then gave a few tears; and then sat in irresponsive silence.

Stung by this apparent want of sympathy, and bewildered by the conviction that a new and heavier misfortune was about to cloud the sky of his life, the young man started up, and standing before the embarrassed girl, said, with much agitation of tone and manner —

"Agnes! how am I to understand this? Are you, too, only a summer friend?"

Scarcely had the words passed from his lips, ere she started to her feet, and glided without a word of answer from the room.

For the space of nearly ten minutes, Heston walked the floor of the apartment in which he had been left alone, every moment expecting the return of his betrothed, but she came not back. At the end of this period he left the house, in so wretched a state of mind, that, for a brief season, he meditated self-destruction. But wiser thoughts restored him to better feelings.

Once more he called to see the yet enthroned idol of his affections; but she refused to meet him, and the idol was cast down and broken into fragments at his feet. It was but gilded clay, and not fine gold, as he had vainly believed.

The effect of this double misfortune was altogether paralyzing. Heston fell into a state of gloomy inaction. Friends urged him to look the world bravely in the face once more, and begin again, with a stout heart, the battle of life. But he answered —

"No — I have been mocked once. Let that suffice. I will not run the risk of another such disaster.

"She is unworthy of a thought," said one, alluding to the maiden who had proved so meanly false to her vows; "and a thousand times unworthy of regret by so true a heart as yours."

"It is easy to say all that," was answered, in a tone of bitterness, "but the heart that once loves, loves on forever — loves, even though the object of affection be proved unworthy."

" Mere poet's talk ! " said the friend. " True love is only based on the perception of qualities. You never truly loved this girl; and time will prove my words. Let her image pass from your thoughts like breath from the face of a mirror. Fling her memory to the winds."

Little effect had this upon the mind of Heston. He held himself aloof from friends, and remained for nearly twelve months a kind of social recluse, brooding over the misfortunes which had so early in life made his sky sunless. As a clerk on a moderate salary, he went through his monotonous round of duties, all interest in the future seeming to have died out of his heart.

At the end of a year there was a gay wedding in the city; gay and imposing enough to create a flutter in certain circles. A young merchant, who had started in business at the same time with Heston, and being more successful, had tried another venture in life, even the doubtful one of leading to the altar a maiden who had been false to her first lover, turning heartlessly from him when the sunshine left his path.

This had the effect to stir into new life the almost dormant energies of our young friend. From that time he walked abroad with a firmer tread, and a countenance more elevated. If his old light-heartedness did not return, he showed a cheerful aspect, and something like a genial side to his character. The true man in him was moving with a new vitality, and throwing off the dead husks of feeling which closed around him closely as cerements.

Ere another year had gone by, an offer to commence business again — or rather, to become a partner in an old established house — was accepted, and he started in the world once more, moving with a steadier step, and with a surer prospect. And he loved again — loved as deeply, and far more wisely — loved one, whose light of love for him was an undying flame, that no waters of misfortune could ever quench.

Morris Heston was all right with the world again; and wiser and happier for the brief but desolating storm which had so sadly marred the beautiful garden of his young life. Prosperity crowned his business efforts, and love made his home a Paradise.

Now and then he met on the street, or in social parties, her who had played him so falsely in his darker hours; never without an almost audibly breathed utterance of thanks for the misfortune which had proved her quality. She was growing yearly into a bold, flaunting, heartless woman of the world; her once beautiful face changing steadily, until, to eyes unveiled by sensuality, it wore a most repellant aspect. To her husband's side, she was rarely seen to move, on social occasions, with an unconscious instinct, as if it was always pleasant to be near him; but plainly preferred any man's company to his.

"Thank God for misfortune!" said Heston, almost speaking aloud, on one occasion, as he saw her turn from her husband with scarcely concealed disgust, and crown another man with a wreath of smiles. "To me it came a blessing in disguise."

It was scarcely a month later, when the husband of this weak, vain, unprincipled woman, returned from his business one evening to find his home desolate, his love hopelessly wrecked, and his baby worse than motherless. His wife had abandoned all her sacred duties, and throwing love, honor, virtue, to the mocking winds, cast her lot with that of a false wretch who lured her from the true path, only to fling her aside after a brief season as a worthless thing.

"Thank God for misfortune!" exclaimed Mr. Heston, in the silence of his swelling heart, when intelligence of this sad event reached his ears. It came to him, first from the lips of his own true wife, who had grown daily dearer to him since the blessed hour when she had given hand and heart together. "Misfortune? Oh, no!" he said. "It was not misfortune — but blessing! The sun was shining still in the sky; only a few clouds had hid from me his loving face."

Almost tearfully did Morris Heston gather his little children into his arms that evening, looking from them to their mother with such loving glances, that half-wondering, and half-joyful, the happy spouse felt a new delight swelling in her heart, that gave a new beauty to her pure countenance.

"I bless God, dear Mary!" said the young man, as she came to his side, drawn by the magnetism of his love, "that you are my wife! My true, loving, faithful wife, and the mother of my precious babes."

Very softly that happy wife and mother laid her lips upon the forehead of her husband, the touch thrilling him to the inmost of his spirit.

Was it misfortune that clouded our young friend's life? No — no. Not misfortune, in the darker sense — the seeming evil was only a blessing disguised. And so, to the right-thinking, the right-feeling, the true-hearted, will all the darker dispensations of life prove themselves blessings. Let us be patient, hopeful, trusting, when the sky is shadowed, nor tremble at the storm that seems desolating the earth. The cloudy tempest is only a transient condition of nature; there is above all, the perpetual sunshine.

To the right-minded there are no misfortunes.

XXI.

THE DEACON'S DREAM.

THERE had always been a pious vein about Deacon Elwood. It showed itself in him when a mere boy. He would play at prayer meeting, if he could get the little ones to join him, while other lads amused themselves with ball or some such worldly pastime. Not that he was less selfish, or more self-denying than his companions. But his fancy led him in this direction, or, perhaps, something more deeply ingrained. It might have been that this pious vein of which we have spoken — not in any lightness, but to indicate a peculiarity — was an intimation of the after life-use for which, in the great complex of uses, he was best fitted by nature.

Be this as it may, young Elwood always showed a

leaning toward the church, and, at an early age, became a member. And it must be said, on his behalf, that, as a young man, he maintained a good character. No one could point to lapses from virtue or integrity, nor even to the follies that so often throw a shade over young men's lives. Fathers pointed him out to their sons as an example.

There was a time when Elwood thought seriously of becoming a minister; and if his father, a money-loving and money-making man, had favored the inclination, he would have been a preacher instead of a trader. But old Mr. Elwood had rather a poor opinion of the pulpit — viewed from a worldly point, and as a profession — and there was enough of the inherited love of money in his son to make him clear sighted as to his father's argument on the subject. So his first love was abandoned for a second and more ardent love.

Still he remained a church-loving man, uniting himself with his brethren in the faith at an early period in life, and standing always in an advanced position. He led in prayer-meetings and other assemblages, and took an active interest in all religious matters. While still a young man, he was chosen to fill the office of deacon. It was a day of pleasing self-congratulation, when news of the appointment reached him. He felt it as a compliment, and yet not an undeserved one. His ambition had looked this way, and it was gratified. "Deacon Elwood." It had a pleasant sound in his ears, "Deacon Elwood." How often it was repeated in his mind for months after the honor crowned his brows — "Deacon Elwood." How many times, as he held pen in hand, did these two words drop down upon white paper, and lie there in his own clear chirography, a pleasant thing to look upon.

In all church matters the deacon was formal, pious, observant and active. With him resided a controlling power in most of the temporalities, as they were called. He was the minister's nearest friend and adviser, and that individual had learned the propriety of humoring him, where no principle of action was involved. In time, Deacon Elwood came to consider himself as not only a pillar in the church, but as equal to a dozen ordinary pillars. He could not see how it was possible, without his active care and watchfulness, for the congregation to be held together. As to his fitness for heaven, that was not a question in the deacon's mind. It had been settled long ago. If he was not a fair subject for heaven, the world was to be pitied. If he didn't pass through the pearly gates in the last time, who, then, would be saved?

But we must come to the deacon's dream. A certain minister, sojourning, had been asked to occupy, for a single time, the pulpit in our deacon's church. Now, it matters not how well a minister may preach, we are very apt to grow inattentive to his positions and arguments, however fairly assumed and lucidly presented, if we listen to him Sabbath after Sabbath for a long time. His words do not come to us with the same clearness of meaning that they did in the beginning, when a certain newness in the man made us hang more earnestly upon what he said. The peculiarities of style that pleased us at first, and even quickened our interest, have come to be felt as tiresome mannerisms. We take his instruction as wide generalities, but rarely understand them in any direct application to our own lives.

This had come to be very much the case with our deacon's minister — at least so far as the deacon was concerned. As to doctrine, he felt himself quite as well posted as the minister; and as to sermonizing, which related mainly to the admonition of sinners, and reproofs of believers for their backslidings and neglect of duties, he had no concern in them, and quite as often spent the church hour in dreaming over his business, as in meditating points of theology.

But a new minister was to fill the pulpit, and Deacon Elwood went to church on that fair Sabbath, with ears quickened for hearing. The sermon was not what is called doctrinal, but practical, and went a little deeper down into a consideration of the life of professors than is usual. Professors being generally regarded as on the safe side, our ministers give their most serious attention to sinners, and try to get them over on to solid ground. On this occasion, however, the saints got a pretty thorough consideration of their case, and it was not, in all respects, flattering to their self-complacency. There were a few sentences that rather disturbed our good deacon's composure, and he took them home with him. Let us consider them as well. The minister said:

"It is not piety that saves a man; there must be charity as well. It isn't love to God alone that opens heaven; there must be genuine love of the neighbor; Sabbath worship, church ordinances, tithes, mint and cummin, will avail nothing to the soul's salvation, if the weightier matters of the law are neglected. Nay, they will be rather as millstones about the neck, to sink your souls to perdition. What are these weightier matters of the law? They are justice and judgment, not external forms of worship. They belong almost entirely to your lives in business and among men, and but remotely, so to speak, to your specifically religious lives. And it is by your states as to the every day life, rather than by your states as to the Sunday life, that you will be judged in the last time. And I solemnly warn you, as God's messenger, to see to it, that the oil of true neighborly love be in your lamps and vessels, when the cry is heard, 'Behold the bridegroom cometh!'

"Let your thought, my dear Christian friends, go forward for a few years — to some of you it may only be a few days — to that time when the eyes of these natural and perishing bodies shall close in darkness, and the inner eyes of the spirit shall open upon the world of eternal verities. When God's angels shall come to you, and looking down through all disguises, explore you as to the quality of your lives — as to your love, as well as your faith. What, my friend," and it seemed to Deacon Elwood as if the preacher looked right at him, as he leaned forward over the pulpit, and spoke in a low, thrilling voice, "do the angels find in the hidden interiors of your life? Love of the neighbor and love of God? or their dark opposites, love of the world and love of self? Do not turn away from the question. It concerns you deeply to know the truth. What affections do most rule in your minds? Take the six days of each week, and from the record of these days answer the question, and, as you value your soul's eternal happiness, answer it faithfully. Heaven is a state of mutual love — a state in which no angel seeks his own good and happiness, but the good and happiness of others. Are you a godly man? Your brethren say yes;

but to be godly is to be God-like. And God is ever seeking to bless others. How is it with you, taking this standard? I press the question. How is it with you, my friend? Are you angel-like and God-like? If not, your external devotion to the church, your good name among the brethren, your pious observances and well-ordered prayers, will help you nothing in that last time when the Lord comes to make up his jewels."

It seemed to Deacon Elwood, as the minister leaned over the pulpit, speaking in a low, penetrating voice, which met no obstruction in the hushed room, that he was speaking to him alone. He had never felt so strangely impressed by a sermon in all his life. One thought, in particular, haunted him: it was that of being examined by the pure angels after death, in regard to the quality of his life. He did not feel altogether satisfied as to the condition in which they would find his more interior affections. The deacon's Sunday dinner was always a good one, and, as his appetite was not very greatly disturbed by the sermon, strongly as some portions of it had taken hold of his thoughts, he did not spare the "creature comforts." After dinner, the Sunday nap succeeded as usual, and in that temporary oblivion as to outward things, came a dream that, while it lasted, proved a most agonizing ordeal to the deacon. We will relate it in his own words:

"I thought," said he, "that my hour had come. But I was tranquil. I had been a church member for a great many years, and had been a servant of the church for nearly the whole of that period. God's grace was my ark of safety. I trusted in my Redeemer. And so, peacefully, I laid myself down and slept, trusting to awake in His righteousness.

"Consciousness came back again, though after how long a period I could not tell. But this I knew — I had passed from the natural to the spiritual world. I lay as one half awakened, or as in a trance, with thought clear, yet with no power of motion. Close by my head sat two angels. I did not see them, but I heard them talking together. They were the angels appointed to attend on my entrance into the spiritual world. The state of my soul was the subject of their conversation. I was soon alive with interest in regard to their judgment. Nothing of what I had done in the world, or thought, or said — nothing as to the doctrines I had believed — was referred to, or considered. It was the state of my affections, or of my 'life's love,' as they called it. They looked into my spirit, searching for neighborly love. A low chill went creeping through my bosom, as I heard a sweet, sad voice murmur —

"'There is only love of the world here.'

"And I knew that it was so; for then I saw myself

as I had never seen myself before. All my life had been one ever out-reaching desire for the things of this world — for its wealth, its natural blessings, and even its honors. All through the six days of each week I had sought *my own* worldly good; and on the Sabbath that crowned the week, sought, in pious acts, to secure *my own* salvation. My neighbor had not been in all my thoughts.

"'Only love of the world,' I heard sighed back by the companion-angel, 'instead of neighborly love.'

"'And if there is only love of the world,' said the angel who had first spoken, 'there can be no love of God; for if a man love not his brother whom he hath seen, how can he love God whom he hath not seen?'

"'Only love of self and love of the world,' sighed the second angel; 'and heaven is a state of love to God and the neighbor. We must depart from him, and let the evil spirits approach who are in a state similar to his own. I thought to have borne this newly-risen soul in joy upwards to the presence of God; but we must leave it to its own.'

"And then I heard them departing. Oh, what anguish of soul was mine! Thus had I wakened to eternal verities. The angels who had been appointed to receive my soul, and bear it heavenward, found in it no heavenly life, and they had left me to the companionship of devils! Now I felt a dark shadow stealing over me. The evil spirits were approaching, and in the horror of the moment I started from sleep."

A thoughtful man was Deacon Elwood for a long time after that alarming vision. Dreams are of various kinds — fantastic, for the most part — yet sometimes of Providence, and significative. The deacon was never in doubt as to the character of his dream. It was the most telling sermon ever addressed to him, and most fruitful in genuine good. He looked down deeper into his heart after that, than he had ever looked before, and understood how gross had been the naturalism in which he had lived, even while self-congratulant on the score of spiritual-mindedness. When the angels appointed to receive his spirit, as it rises into the eternal world at death, examine him as to his quality, may they find that true love of God and the neighbor which alone makes heaven.

XXII.

WOULD YOU HAVE IT OTHERWISE?

TWO men met on the public highway, stopped, clasped hands, and looked at each other for some moments, without speaking. The face of one of them was worn, exhausted, and shaded by trouble; that of the other calm, elevated, and full of sympathetic life.

"I thought you were triple guarded," said the calm-faced man.

"And I was," replied the other. "Human prudence could do no more. I saw where other men were weak or foolish, and took warning. I never acted from impulse; never let a too eager desire for gain betray me into unsafe lines of business. I built on solid foundations. And yet, for all this, I am little else than a beggar to-day. It is hard, Mr. Melville! And I feel a sense of wrong. What have I done, to be thus punished? I can show a fair record. No man can ever say that I ever overreached him in business; nor any poor man that I have withheld his wages, or oppressed him in any thing. I have been just and honorable in my dealings, which cannot be said of many who still count their wealth by tens of thousands. Talk of Providence ruling for good in the world! I am not able to see it clearly."

"But you will see it," answered the one who had been addressed as Mr. Melville. "The dust and smoke of falling and consuming fortune, have blinded your eyes."

"I shall never see the justice that lies in an almost wanton destruction of my house, while my neighbor's, every brick of which is cemented to its fellows by some wrong deed, stands scatheless."

"You state your view of the case broadly, Mr. Andrews."

"Yet with exact truth," was answered.

"A year hence, and, in re-stating the case, you will omit the term wanton."

"No sir! That is wanton which looks to no good end."

"If good is not regarded, then evil must be the inspiring motive," said Mr. Melville. "And so, in refer-

10

ring your misfortune to Providence, you charge God with evil."

"I leave you, as a clergyman, to settle that point," replied Mr. Andrews, with signs of impatience. "I am unable to see beyond the circle in which I stand. Six months ago, I was in the enjoyment of a handsome property, honestly acquired, through years of patient labor in a useful calling. To-day I stand stripped of everything. If not a sparrow falls unnoted to the ground — if the very hairs of our head are numbered — all this must have reached me through the permissions, if not the ordinations, of Providence. So you read the event, I am sure."

"So I read it, Mr. Andrews."

"And God is good and just?"

"Essentially good and just."

"Expound the riddle then."

"I may give you the clue by which to expound it for yourself. Undoubting convictions only come to us as the result of experience. After we have lived through our disciplinary states, we rise to higher spiritual elevations, thus gaining a clearer atmosphere, and a wider range of vision. Now, you are feeling around you with uncertain hands, in the obscurity of a deep and narrow valley; but out of this hindering state, you will surely rise, and see the broad fields rich with an eternal verdure that your stronger hands may reap, and mountains bathed in heaven's own sunlight, to whose summits you will have strength to climb. The clue I offer is in this proposition, the truth of which is as clear to me as sunlight: The purposes of God, in all His Providential dealings with man, have regard to his spiritual well being, and look to his eternal happiness in heaven ; *and to this end, all natural events are made subservient.* If continued worldly prosperity will best aid in the implantation of germs of spiritual life, and stimulate their growth, then worldly misfortunes will not come ; but if sorrows, troubles, or losses are needed, these, in tender mercy, will be sent. So far as my observation goes, the sunshine of worldly prosperity is not favorable to the growth of a divine life in the human soul. It dries the seed, and burns up the tender shooting plants ; or so stimulates the growth of noxious weeds, that they spring up with a rank vitality and choke the heavenly verdure."

Mr. Andrews bent his head and listened. There was a pause, but he did not answer.

"I will not press the subject now," said the clergyman. "Take the clue I have given, and by means thereof search for the higher truths to which it will lead. *God regards eternal ends*. Fix that in your thought. Dwell upon it. Try to understand the immortal, the eternal interests it involves; and, in the effort, light will descend into your mind. God is our father, and, as a father, will never permit pain to reach us except as a warning against soul-destroying evils, even as pain of body warns us of the encroachments of diseases that would destroy its life."

The two men parted. Mr. Andrews took with him the clue his minister had given. At first he could not hold it steadily. It would drop from his hand and seem lost. But, conscious that he was in a wilderness, out of which no blind reasonings of his own could extricate him, he would grapple after the clue, and, when found again, hold it with a firmer grasp.

"Eternal ends." Often he found himself repeating the words, while thought lifted itself now upward into purer regions, or went searching down into his heart, turning over motives and purposes, and discovering in many lurking places hidden things of selfishness that could not stand unabashed in the pure light of Christian truth. He had been for years building his house upon the sands, and now he began to see how uncertain were the foundations.

A year afterwards. Let us see how the discipline of misfortune has wrought with Mr. Andrews. Let us see whether he has kept hold of the clue, and whether it has led him out of the bewildering maze in which he found himself. The time is evening. He is sitting, with his eyes on a book. The apartment is small, plainly furnished, but neat. A woman comes in, with a work-basket in her hand, and placing it on a table, sits down near him. He lifts his eyes and looks at her a moment or two, with a gentle smile of welcome on his lips, and then drops them again on the page before him. The face of the woman is peaceful, and yet, in her eyes, and around her lips, you can see the signs of past suffering. A little while, and then both look up and listen. A few moments, and the door is opened.

"Mr. Melville!" The voices that greet the minister are full of welcome.

"I was thinking of you but an instant ago," fell from the lips of Mr. Andrews.

"Our thoughts often go before us, and announce our coming," is answered.

A pleasant exhilaration of mind follows. Mr. Andrews is smiling and cheerful, and his wife leans and listens with consenting interest as her husband and the minister fall into conversation.

"I think," said Mr. Melville, during the progress of this conversation, "that you kept firm hold of the clue I gave months ago, and that it has enabled you to find the way out of labyrinthine doubt into sunny regions."

"I see things very differently to day," was answered.

"Consider my question closely. Wonld you have it otherwise than it is?"

"Otherwise?"

"Strike, in your thought, the balance of loss and gain. Are you better off, or worse off, than you were a year ago!"

Mr. Andrews dropped his eyes, and began pondering the question. He understood the higher meanings that were in Mr. Melville's mind.

"How are your mental states?"

"More peaceful!"

"And your heart?"

"Not so wedded to the things of this world, which are forever changing, alluring, disappointing."

"Things more satisfying are yours. Truths, the full acknowledgment of which lifts you into regions of angelic thought, and the life of which introduces you into angelic companionship. You are happier than you were?"

"I am in greater tranquillity. Life has deeper satisfactions. And I can see farther beyond. Accumulated wealth, with an ever-growing desire to make larger and still larger accumulations, walled me around, and shut away from my vision the world of richer beauty I now see, and towards which I am trying to walk."

"In striking the balance, then, the larger figures are on the side of gain."

"Yes, if the things of the spirit are of more value than the things of sense."

"And they are. So far outside of all comparison are worldly riches and spiritual riches, that between them we can hardly say there is a relation of values.

> "'Wisdom divine ! Who tells the price
> Of wisdom's costly merchandise ?
> Wisdom to silver we prefer,
> And gold is dross compared to her.'

No external change ; no robbery ; no commercial disaster can touch this wealth. It is ours in spite of all that men can do. God, in his Providence, does not suffer it to be wasted ; but all his dealings with the children of men are to the end that it may be stored up in their minds for use ; and in using it they have undying felicities. But returning to my question — Would you have it otherwise than it is ? Would you take back the fortune that dropped from your possession a year ago, if, with that fortune, your old mental and moral states must also be restored ?"

For a little while Mr. Andrews leaned his head in thought. Then looking up, he pronounced an emphatic —

"No."

"God knows best," said the minister. Too wise to err, too good to be unkind, all his Providences are in love. It is our misjudgment that questions their origin and ends. We set our hearts on natural things that perish in the using — that almost always disturb or create inordinate desires, which grow more clamorous with every gain. But God's regard for these never goes beyond their service of a more interior life; and he permits their enjoyment, or not, as giving or withholding may serve the higher ends. Would He be good, and wise, and merciful were this not so? Who does not blame the weak parent who indulges the natural inclinations of his children, to the destruction of those unselfish and noble qualities that give to matured life the beauty and strength of a well disciplined manhood? Shall God be more foolish in dealing with His children during their probationary minority in this world? If we call evil good, He will not. You say 'No,' you would not have it otherwise than it is. In what marked respect is it better with you than it was before?"

"Briefly, in this: I was a church member. I desired to live as a Christian man. I looked to heaven as my eternal dwelling place after life's fitful fever. But, interiorly, I was selfish and worldly minded. All my thoughts revolved around myself. In my eager pursuit of riches, imagination toyed with possession and built grand castles for poor natural life to dwell in. It was self — self — self. There was rarely a thought of stewardship. For me the sun shone, the grass grew, the landscape spread itself in beauty. I became colder and colder toward our common humanity; and from living the bad precept, 'every man for himself,' began confirming it as a right axiom. Thus it was with me when a good Providence removed the worldly blessings that I was using to the destruction of my soul; for, if to the end of life, I had so kept on, turning myself away from humanity and from God, could I have risen, at death, into heaven? I fear not!"

"So the discipline which was so bitter at first, gives sweetness now?"

"Yes. And though poorer than a year ago, I am richer in the more perfect enjoyment of what things I have, and my future is luminous with brighter hopes."

"God's ways are not as our ways," said Mr. Melville.

"But they are the true ways, and lead to heavenly felicities," was the peaceful answer.

XXIII.

IN THE HEREAFTER.

" Not as a child shall we again behold her."

HALL I know him in Heaven?

With what a yearning, almost passionate desire to penetrate the secrets of the world beyond, did Mrs. Harding ask this question. The beautiful had died, and left her soul desolate. The light of her life had gone out, and she sat in darkness. "Shall I know my sweet boy in Heaven?" On the answer to this question, all hope in the future seemed resting.

"He will grow up into the beauty and stature of a man-angel," said one, in answer. "Unless God should call you early, not as a child may you again behold him."

"Not as a child!" A flash of pain quivered suddenly among the shadows which lay darkly on Mrs. Harding's face. "Oh, no, no, no! I cannot believe that! My darling will wait for his mother. I must find him as I lost him. God is not so cruel."

"She sat with lips parted, like one in fear. The friend resumed —

"He will grow in Heaven. Think, my dear friend — must it not be so? As his tender soul receives knowledge, will it not enlarge? and the new body, of spiritual and immortal substance, with which the soul clothes itself, grow in corresponding stature? In the laws of our natural life, we see only a representation of the laws of a higher and spiritual life. Turn away your thoughts from grief, and let the light of reason penetrate your mind. Into sorrow, an element of blinding selfishness is almost sure to come. It is of ourselves, and our loss, that we think. But we must rise, in a degree, superior to this state, before we can see and accept the great truth, that, in God's eyes, all souls are equal, and each soul destined for its own peculiar place, and designed for its own peculiar work in the universe. Heaven, into which your child has arisen, is not a condition of aimless enjoyment, but of active service. Use is the great celestial law, that, like gravitation, holds everything in order and beautiful consistence. As he grows and develops into an angel, the Master

Builder will lift him to the place he is designed to occupy in the living temple of God. Accept it as a truth, my dear friend, that, in dying young, and growing to spiritual manhood in Heaven, he will be more truly fitted for the place he is designed to fill through the eternal ages."

Thought began to stir in the mind of the bereaved one. She bent forward listening.

"A mother's love is the purest, and tenderest, and most devoted of all loves," resumed the friend. Then she added, dwelling with significant emphasis on the words — "*in the beginning.*"

"Always, and forever!" was answered quickly — almost indignantly.

"A mother's love, with all of its unspeakable depths and yearning tendernesses, is only God's love in her heart, given for the protection and care of offspring. It is seen in the evil, as well as in the good. Nay! do not hold up your hands in rejection; but reflect! Is not the mother's love a different emotion in the hour when she receives a feeble, helpless babe upon her bosom, from what it is when the boy goes forth to school, or the man steps out into the world, to take his place among men? Her interest and affection do not die; but love is of a different quality. Why is this?"

The mother looked bewildered. She did not answer.

"Your mother loved you, when you lay a helpless babe in her arms, as fondly as you loved him who was bone of your bone, and flesh of your flesh. If that love is, to-day, what it was twenty-five years ago, has your response been adequate? Have you done to it no violence? But, it is not the same; and, therefore, even though your heart turned from her, and rested in a more passionate and absorbing love for a husband, and in a tenderer than any filial love, upon your own child, yet did not a shadow fall over her serene brow. Her love had grown larger, and more unselfish. She had no jealous pangs. Her own life, separating itself daily, more and more from all hindering entanglements with other lives, is growing more and more perfect in that just individuality, which gives to each part its highest relation of use to the whole."

"Her life is a saintly life," said the mourner. "All women are not like my mother."

"Is not her life a true life?"

"Yes — yes."

"And, are not all lives that fall away from her saintly standard, just so far inadequate — false lives?"

"It may be so."

"Did your mother ever lose a babe?"

"Yes; a little sister died in the opening of her third summer. Your question brings back the memory of that event with a strange vividness."

"Did she grieve for her lost one?"

"Oh yes, wildly. I was but a child at the time, yet can I never forget the intensity of my mother's sorrow."

"It seemed to you excessive?"

"I own that it did. But, how could a child comprehend a mother's feelings? I see it differently now."

"It was like yours, a natural sorrow," said the friend, "and passed, in time, as yours will pass, giving place to that purified love of the departed, which sees them as goodly stones, builded into the temple of the living God. Natural loves are for this world only, and rest on persons and appearances; but spiritual loves are based on spiritual affinities, and have relation to interior likenesses, assimilations and consanguinities."

"And shall we not make up families in Heaven?" was asked, in a tone of surprise. "Will not my mother find there the child she lost so many years ago? Is not my father waiting for her?— and my brother, who left her just as his manly tread passed bravely out into the world?"

"If there be in you spiritual as well as natural consanguinities, yes. But of this, only God knows. Of one thing we may be sure; if we love what is true, and do what is good, we shall pass, at death, into the company of those who love and do similar truth and good, and be supremely happy with them in performing the Lord's work through the ages of eternity. And what is true of us, will be true of all who lead good lives in the sight of God. These natural loves, which are given to us for blessing and safety in this world, terminate, I think, with the closing of natural life."

"No!—no!—no! I will not believe it! Such a doctrine shocks me to the very centre of my being." And the mother turned away from her friend.

"You must rise into a higher perception of the meaning of a single life before you can understand this matter," said the friend. "In each life, there is a selfhood peculiarly its own — an individuality that makes the quality of its thought and affection different from that of all other lives existing or possible to exist. In a word, no two human souls ever were, or ever can be, identically the same. Born from the infinite source of life, there must be infinite variety. But, as there exist genera and species in the lower forms of nature, so do these exist in the higher spiritual creation of human souls. Every distinct individual of a species holds likeness and relationship with its genera; and, in like manner does every soul distinct in itself, hold a likeness and relation to other souls, and act with them, for use, in some organ or part of the grand man of Heaven. Each is a centre of peculiar life and influence, yet reciprocal in giving and receiving, and acting in just harmony with the general law."

The mother did not answer, but thought was again active.

"See," continued the friend, "how, as men advance in years, and their minds grow into maturing vigor, each one separates himself more and more from his first natural relations, and etablishes a new relation for himself, based on the organic peculiarities of his own mind, as differing from all other minds. Will it be less so in the case of those who pass from the world, to develop in Heaven?"

"And so," said the mourner, looking with sad, dreary eyes, into the face of her friend, "you have only this consolation to offer, that my boy will grow up to angelic manhood in Heaven, and forget his mother?"

The friend did not reply. "How is it possible," such were her thoughts, "for me to lift her mind into a perception of this truth, that each soul is destined for some high and holy office, in the performance of which the happiness received will be in proportion to the good that is done?" After a brief silence, she said, her tones softening —

"You love him very much?"

Eyes swimming in tears, were the mother's answer.

"And desire his supremest happiness?"

"Oh, yes."

"And that must come in Heaven, whither our good Lord has translated him. I do not think, even now, that you would take him back, were it in your power, into this world of sorrow and pain."

"I do not ask to receive him back. My love is not so selfish as that. Oh, no, no! Dear babe! I give him to the angels. But, may I not find him again? May I not once more take him into my arms? That is the question. Ah, my friend, your answers to this question do not bring hope or consolation. They say — You have lost your babe forever!"

"Have you not rather found him forever?" said the friend.

There was no answer, but a look of surprise.

"If he had lived, and grown up in this world, would you not have lost your babe? The baby would have died in the boy; the boy in the youth; the youth in the man. Now, love may hold the precious one forever to your heart. If you live here until fourscore, you may, at any time, fold back the curtain of memory, and look into the cradle where infancy smiles. Grief will be lost in the passage of years, but a holy tenderness, full of sweetness and tranquillity, will remain. Of all your children, should the rest be spared, his memory will be most precious. Looking down into my own heart, I speak of what I do know."

"But, for all that, he will not remain a babe," said the mother. "He will grow up into the stature of an angel."

"Yes."

"And cease to think of her who bore him."

"Just in the degree that you, in heavenly uses and the delights springing therefrom, will forget, in the cycles of eternity, your mother, and she the mother on whose bosom she once lay in the helplessness of infancy. God has work for all his children; for you and for me; for your babe called early to heaven, as well as for my babe who went there many years ago. Let us be glad in heart, my friend, that we have been called to the high office of increasing, even by one addition, the heaven of angels. Picture to yourself a pure and wise being, forever active in good deeds; forever seeking to impart happiness to others; forever ministrant to tempted and sorrowing ones here, or adding to the delights of heaven, and then think: — 'In my body that being had life!' Does not the thought send a thrill of strange gladness through your soul? It does. I see it by the clearer light in your eyes. I see it in the serener expression of your face. Nay — nay! You would not have your baby wait in helpless infancy, through the long period that may pass ere your time of removal come, in order that you may clasp him, as a baby, again to your heart. A truer and a purer love desires to see him a man-angel, nobly fulfilling the laws of angelic life."

"I will think of all this," said the mourner, speaking more calmly. "You have led me up to a place from which I have a wider range of vision. Some things assume different aspects and relations. I may have been very selfish, very limited in my feelings. But, I pray God to give me light and comfort in this deep sorrow. I would be patient and submissive. Ah, yes; — It is a high thought that you have given me. — And shall I, in the weakness of a mother's love, desire to hold my boy back from his true life, rather than in its strength to ask for him growth and development, even to the stature and powers of eternal manhood in heaven? No — no! Let me rise above this weakness of sorrow, and put on its strength."

By true thoughts we are lifted out of darkened states. But, these states return again. Thought folds its wings, letting us sink into the obscurity from which we had arisen. But, we remember the higher regions, the broader vision, and the serener atmosphere in which we breathed, and, after awhile, uplift our wings, and try once more to reach the upper air. We gain it. How much clearer the sight than before! What seemed obscure, or confused, in the first ascent, now stands forth in well defined aspect. Accepting the lessons of truth, even though in some violence to natural affection, we do not recede into such deep obscurity, when we sink to the level of actual states again; but see clearer, and rest on the truths we have seen.

So it was with our stricken mother, who, in the beginning of her sorrow, refused to be comforted. Her friend had lifted her into a region of thought unattained till now : — had given her views never before suggested. They did not afford her the assurance for which her soul was craving; the comfort she asked; but they gave her glimpses of a broader plan in the creation of human souls than she had ever conceived.

"Thy will, not mine be done," she murmured, lifting her eyes upwards, as she pondered when alone, all that her friend had spoken. And even as she said this, the mantle of peace was gathered, by angel hands, around her soul. Still, love's deep yearning was not suppressed; and still the heart asked, "Shall I know him in heaven?"

That night, a dream held her through all the long watches. She was sitting in sorrow by the empty cradle of her boy, when a stranger entered the room, and said, "Come. You shall go to your lost one." No awe oppressed her. Rising, with hope and joy in her heart, she followed the stranger. They journeyed for what seemed a long time, first passing through dark forests and deep valleys; and then through fair landscapes, gradually ascending, widening and increasing in beauty, until they reached a city so fair to look upon, that its splendor oppressed her soul. The walls were of precious stones, the gates of pearl, and the streets of pure gold. As she moved along the crystalline pavements, she saw houses and palaces of wondrous design and proportions, such as no mortal conception had ever reached. Into one of the grandest of these she entered with her guide, passing under vast porticos borne up by jasper columns, and along halls and corridors that stretched to interminable distances.

"Here," spoke the attendant, "first come all infants who die in the world," and as he said this, the mother found herself in a wide chamber, the air of which was full of sweet odors, and tremulous with low music, to which her heart leaped in tender responses. That odor was from the breath of infants; and the music that filled the room was the harmonious mingling of baby voices. As she entered, a beautiful maiden came to meet her. Lovingly she held to her bosom the babe that mother had lost a little while before.

"Oh, give him to me!" cried the mother, eagerly stretching out her hands.

"Will you take him back?" said the maiden, as she laid the baby in her arms.

"Mine! mine!" exclaimed the mother, in an ecstasy of joy, as she clasped her lost one almost wildly to her heart.

"And God's," answered the maiden, gently yet reverently. "You were chosen by Him to this great honor."

A new impulse stirred in the mother's heart. Love lost nothing of its intensity, but was elevated. Selfish affection died, and in her whole being she felt the motions of a higher life.

"Shall I keep this babe all to myself," she said, in her heart. "Shall I take him back to a world of pain and trouble, when his presence here gives a new pulse of joy to heaven? No — no! That would be selfishness, not love. Chosen by God to this great honor! Oh, life, life! What a blessing, if only for this!"

"You will not take him back," said the maiden, with a smile of ineffable sweetness.

The mother laid the babe softly on the maiden's bosom, kissed him, and turned away. As she did so, her attendant led her out by an open door, and they passed through palaces, fields, and groves. The time was long and the distance great. Years seemed to elapse. At last they came to a large building, grandly beautiful in its architecture, and rising in the midst of a garden. Entering, she found it to be a hall of instruction, in which pupils with their teachers were assembled.

"Here," said the attendant, "youths, who have grown up from infancy in heaven, are taught. The mind does not change in its character by death. Translation from the natural to the spiritual world cannot, in itself, make any soul wiser. Instruction in spiritual sciences and knowledges is as needful here, as instruction in natural sciences and knowledges in the lower world. For this reason, the young are taught in schools by wise and loving instructors."

The mother stood in a wide hall, in which were many groups of children, gathered around their teachers, and listening to the words that fell from their lips with the most earnest and pleased attention. Soon, all the groups, or classes, arranged themselves, by a spontaneous movement, into a single group, and one who was chief of the instructors stood forth and said —

"Our theme to-day has been Heavenly Happiness. In what does it consist?"

A youth, tender in years, but with pure thought written on his white forehead, away from which the hair fell back in luxuriant curls, arose amid his companions and answered —

"Heavenly happiness is the delight of use.'"

"And what is the delight of use?" asked the instructor.

"That interior joy which always comes into the soul, when good is done from a love of good."

"Whence does it come?"

"From the Lord, who is the bestower of all good," answered the youth.

Then it was given the mother to know, that he who thus answered was her own son — not now a babe, but in the blossom of advancing years; growing in intelligence and wisdom, towards the stature of an angel. And he came to her, after the school had closed, and tenderly looking at her said —

"Oh, life is a blessing; and blessed are they through whom God gives life."

There followed another long journey amid scenes of ineffable beauty and grandeur, occupying a period that would have been, in time, the aggregate of years. Then was entered a temple where one taught, and the words that fell from his lips were in sentences of wisdom, such as only the wisest and best of angels had power to utter. And they who hearkened, hung with rapt interest on his words. When the discourse was over, the audience went out, talking together of what they had heard, and the mother listened to their speech, and knew as she listened, that the wise teacher of whom they spake, was once a babe on her bosom. And as this knowledge came, the teacher stood by her side. The sweetness of his countenance filled her with unspeakable delight. It seemed as if heaven's own sunshine were falling into her soul. Bending, with a loving grace, he said —

"We are the children of God, when born into heaven; and in doing His work, receive the blessedness of heaven. All souls are His — yours, mine — and for each He has work that shall not fail in all the eternal ages, — work, in the doing of which perpetual joy is born. Make yourself ready for this work in a patient, trusting submission to His will, and in deeds of love to His children. He will make up your jewels."

The vision passed, and it was morning. Those who had looked upon the grieving mother's countenance when the day went out in a darkness not so deep as that which enshrouded her spirit, wondered at its calmness and elevation. But she spoke not of the vision, though its influence rested upon her soul like a peaceful benediction.

XXIV.

SHE WENT AWAY WITH THE ANGELS.

"LITTLE Nellie Winter is dead!" said a neighbor, coming hurriedly into Mrs. Grover's sitting room. There was a look of grief in her face, and her eyes were full of tears.

"Dead!" and the work fell into Mrs. Grover's lap. "Dead! Poor Mary Winter! it will break her heart. That child was her idol."

"She was a dear little girl," said the neighbor. "Too good to live in this world, I have often thought. Did you never notice, Mrs. Grover, what a strange sweetness played sometimes about her mouth."

"Yes, I have often observed, and spoken of it."

"And there was something very uncommon in the way she looked out of her eyes. Some people's eyes look straight forward, some a little downward, and some restlessly from side to side; but Nellie's large, clear, blue eyes seemed always looking upwards, and there was an expression in them as if they had visions not revealed to grosser sight."

"Have you seen Mary?" asked Mrs. Grover.

"No; Aunty Granger came by our house just now, and told me of Nellie's death. I must run back, and put on my things, and go over immediately."

"Call for me," said Mrs. Grover. "I will get ready and go with you. Poor Mary! I dread to see her."

The neighbors parted, but were together again in less than ten minutes, and on their way to visit a sister in affliction.

"I wonder how she bears it? What did Aunty Granger say?"

"Nothing, as to that. She merely brought me word, and then hurried away. She said that Nellie died about two hours ago, and that she had been helping to lay her out."

"Well, I know how to feel for Mary," said the neighbor, in a sorrowful voice. "I've lost children, and know what a heart-breaking thing it is. Talking to one does no good. They talked to me — ministers, and friends, and all; but they might as well have talked to the wind."

"Mary Winter has a great deal of fortitude, and she is a true Christian woman," remarked Mrs. Grover.

"I think her a little cold," was replied to this.

"May it not be that she has schooled her feelings into submission?"

"Perhaps so, I cannot tell. We are not all alike; but if Mary can bear this trouble calmly, she is made of sterner stuff than common mortals. An eye plucked out gives intensest pain."

And so the two neighbors talked, until they came to the door on which hung the sign of death, when they were silent. A moment or two they paused on the threshhold, and then passed in. The door opened directly into Mrs. Winter's small parlor, or best room, as she modestly called it. Gentle hands had already done the work of preparation for the grave: and there lay the pure body of the departed one, wrapped in snowy garments. A few friends were in the room, and all were standing near the body, gazing in silence upon the dead face, that looked like an exquisite piece of sculpture. There was no harsh or repellant aspect in the countenance — nothing that chilled you with a mortal coldness; but only a look of Heavenly sweetness. Death had done his work with a gentle hand.

From the little parlor, Mrs. Grover and her companion went to the chamber where the stricken mother had retired. Their visit was not one of vulgar intrusion. It was prompted by true womanly sympathy. The curtains were drawn, and the room in shadow, but not darkened. Two neighbors were sitting with Mrs. Winter, and from the look on all their faces, it was evident they had been conversing. The mother's eyes were full of tears, but her countenance was rather elevated than depressed. She reached her hand to the new comers, and even smiled faintly as she greeted them.

Mrs. Grover pressed the hand of Mrs. Winter, and looked tenderly in her face, but did not venture a word; the neighbor who had accompanied her said, in a voice broken with feeling,

"Oh, Mary! this is very sad; my heart aches for you. Death is a terrible thing."

"It is hard for those who are left behind." Her voice trembled, and tears fell over her cheeks; yet did not the smile around her lips fade wholly away.

"And it is hard, also, for those who go away," answered the neighbor, without reflection. "Oh, the doubt and darkness, the uncertainty of that unknown voyage into eternity, which every soul, small or great, must take alone. I shudder to think of it."

"Not alone," said Mrs. Winter, impressively, "not alone. God is too full of tender compassion for his children, to let one of them go unattended over the river of death. I knew that dear Nellie went away with the angels, for I felt their holy presence in the last hour, and when the eyes of my child looked their last look on my face, I knew that they opened upon the inner world, and rested serenely on the countenances of Heavenly attendants."

Tears were running over the face of Mrs. Winter, as she said this. Her pious faith, while it threw a shining bridge over the abyss that lies between earth and Heaven, and took away all painful thoughts of her child, did not exclude from her heart the anguish of bereavement. She was human.

"Went away with the angels," said the neighbor, as if struck with the words. She spoke half to herself; "Oh, if one could believe that."

"It is with me no matter of dim faith, but a confident assurance," answered Mrs. Winter. "The spiritual world, into which we go on leaving this outer state of being, is a world of real things, and peopled like this; for have not untold millions gone into it? And can I believe anything else than that, when one is passing upward to the great company of angels, God commissions some of them to receive the pure spirit, as it emerges into their world? It is easy for me to believe this — impossible to believe the opposite. Yes, yes, dear Nellie went away with the angels, and is with them now."

"I went there hoping to speak a comforting word to Mary," said the neighbor, as she walked homeward, "but, instead, the mourner has spoken comfort to my own heart. Ah, Mrs. Grover, that thought of going alone into the world beyond — of my timid, shrinking child's going alone, and meeting the terrors of death, has haunted me like a spectre. But, Mary Winter's confident assurance that Nellie went away attended by angels, is already taking shape in my mind, and giving to it a new balance; I see dimly, yet it is true that it must be so."

"It must be so of tender, innocent children," said Mrs. Grover. "And if true of children, why not true of every soul that rises into the spiritual world, which is not a vast chimerian wildness, but a world of perfect order and beauty. We think, as a general thing, too sadly of death, and invest it with unreal terrors, when at most it is a simple passage of the human soul into its higher and more perfect sphere of life. The sadness and fear should only have reference to an evil and corrupt heart, for the death is indeed a sad completion of that portion of life in which the after condition is fixed to eternity. But when little children, and good men and women die, we need not weep at their change, for they have only gone from us in company with angels."

XXV.

THE WINE OF LIFE.

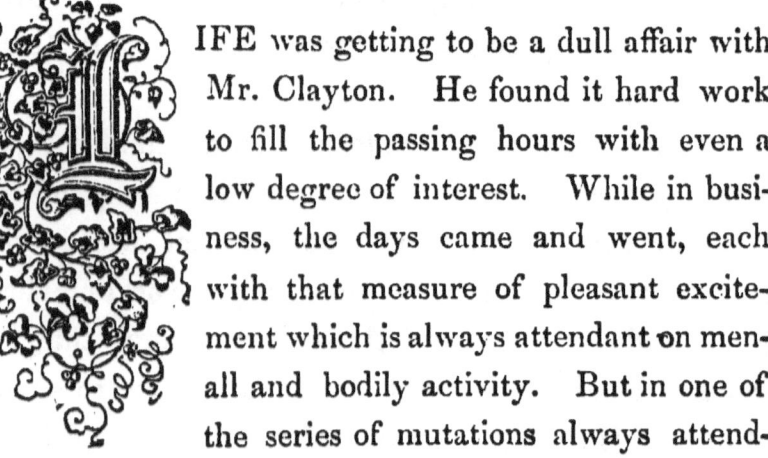LIFE was getting to be a dull affair with Mr. Clayton. He found it hard work to fill the passing hours with even a low degree of interest. While in business, the days came and went, each with that measure of pleasant excitement which is always attendant on mental and bodily activity. But in one of the series of mutations always attendant on human life, Mr. Clayton found himself ruled out of business, and left, with a small competence, idle.

Thirty thousand dollars were paid to Mr. Clayton in cash, as his share of profit. In less than a week afterwards he had received over half a dozen proposals to re-enter business. Some from established firms in want of capital, and some from ambitious young men, whose position as salesmen in extensive establishments gave them, as they supposed, large ability to control custom. But to all of these Mr. Clayton turned an indifferent ear.

"A bird in the hand is worth two in the bush," he said to himself, as he looked calmly at his bank account. "I'll put this beyond the reach of danger, and then take mine ease."

Between two and three months of pleasant excitement were passed in the work of settling the basis of his future income, a period of real enjoyment to our retired merchant. A new life seemed to flow through his veins. The mill-horse routine of daily duties was changed for a state of freedom to go out and come in at his own good pleasure; and Mr. Clayton often pitied the old business acquaintances whom he met occasionally hurrying along the street, with shut, earnest lips and care-contracted brows. He felt himself to them as the freed courser in a wide and grassy meadow, to the toiling beast, dragging wearily at his load.

But there came another state of mind. After completing his investments, Mr. Clayton had nothing else to do; and soon, when morning broke, his thought began to reach forward through the day with a vague searching disquietude. For books he had little taste; for art less. Politics had no charm for one of his temperament. He voted with his party, more from habit and prejudice than from reason and principle. This done, he left matters of public interest to take care of themselves — at least, so far as he was concerned.

A year of leisure had been enjoyed, and life, as we said in the beginning, was getting to be a dull affair with Mr. Clayton. His mind, like a stagnant pool, was beginning to breed unsightly and noxious things. He was growing crotchetty, strangely self-willed, unreasonable, and ill-tempered at home, so that his wife and orphan niece — he had no children — were having an uncomfortable time with him. Mr. Clayton was not philosopher enough to understand his own case. He did not know that, even to evil men, states of tranquillity and interior satisfaction come as the reward of useful work; nor that the good feel disquietude whenever they fold their arms in voluntary idleness. It had not occurred to him that the mind was a beautiful and highly complicated machine, that must be kept in orderly motion, or rust and damage ensue. No, Mr. Clayton was a dull thinker. He lacked enthusiasm. From quick moving thoughts the light of perception was not evolved.

One day, after exhaling certain noxious things, bred in the stagnant pools of his mind, arousing his wife to anger, and hurting his dependent niece, so that she resolved, and even threatened, to leave his house, Mr. Clayton strayed forth, an aimless and an unhappy man, to kill the hours until it should be time to return to dinner.

The dinner bell did not ring for some minutes after the arrival of Mr. Clayton at home. Taking up a newspaper, he commenced running his eyes along the colums for something of interest. This paragraph arrested his attention. "The very thing that men need in life is some satisfying and exalting element, that shall give heroism and elevation to the affairs of daily life. We live in the midst of vulgarities, little petty troubles, a thousand mechanical things that have not much juice in them. The greater part of our life is spent in contact with things that have little in themselves to reward our sensibility. We must, therefore, have something in the soul to make them glorious."

At almost any other time this would have been to Mr. Clayton as if uttered in a dead language. He would have perceived no meaning in it whatever. Now it was a gleam of light.

"Heaven knows," he said, speaking to himself, and with sufficient mental energy to stir his heart with stronger pulses — "Heaven knows that I want some satisfying and exalting element to give heroism and elevation to the things of *my* daily life."

After dinner Mr. Clayton did not fall to sleep in his chair — now a common habit — and doze away an hour or two. His thoughts had been set in motion, and kept on with sufficient velocity to overcome all inclination to drowsiness. About four o'clock word came to him that a gentleman had called — Mr. Walker, a person who had asked for him in the morning.

On meeting this gentleman, Mr. Clayton recognized him as one often seen on the street in public places, but never personally identified.

"I have come," he said, coming at once to the object of his visit, "to see if I cannot interest you in a matter that every good citizen and Christian man should have at heart. A few of us, painfully alive to the condition of a large number of little children in this part of the city, who are abandoned or neglected by their parents, and consequently growing up in ignorance and vice, have determined to found an institution, if possible, for their asylum and instruction. We have already procured funds, rented a house, and employed a matron and assistants. Twenty children, boys and girls, have been taken from the street, and are now comfortably clothed, fed and instructed. Now, what we want, Mr. Clayton, is a man of leisure who will give a few hours of each day to the supervision of this important charity. I am engaged in business, and, however much my heart may be in the thing, cannot assume so important a duty. The same is true of others who are acting with me.

This morning a gentleman suggested your name, and I have called to see if we cannot interest you in the cause."

"Suppose," said Mr. Walker, ere the response came, "that you go round with me to our rooms, and see what we are doing. They are in the neighborhood. I'm sure you will be interested."

"I will do so," answered Mr. Clayton, accepting the opportunity to postpone a decision that he was not yet prepared to make. He did not feel like saying no, and was far from being inclined to say yes.

Mr. Clayton was, naturally, a kind-hearted man. Enough was shown him at the asylum to touch his sympathies, awaken his interest, and give to his stimulated mental powers the element of heroism. It took but little persuasion on the part of three or four intelligent citizens, who were present, and under engagement to meet weekly at the rooms for conference, to lead Mr. Clayton to accept the important office of daily visitor and overseer of a nursery for human souls, abandoned but for this refuge to the coils of the Wicked One.

There was no more weariness of mind after this — no more beatings about of thought, oppressed with its own burden of inactivity — no more sourness of spirit. Mr. Clayton was a live man again, with all his powers active. Under his thoughtful supervision, seconded by gentlemen of wealth and active benevolence, the institution grew rapidly, and soon, from sheltering and training for useful lives twenty little ones, gathered over one hundred within its protecting walls.

"We owe much of all this success in our plans to you," said Mr. Walker, one day, while he sat with Mr. Clayton reviewing the items in an annual report. "For lack of one who could give to an asylum a daily superintendence, and hold in charge its general interests, all things were inefficient, and we had even talked of abandoning a charity which it seemed impossible rightly to sustain. But, we found you in the day of our despondency; and under your diligent care, zeal for the cause of humanity and self-devotion, have been able to effect the ends which lay so near to our hearts. What human arithmetic can give us the sum of good to flow from this successful effort!"

Idler and ease-taker — man of wealth and leisure, whose days drag heavily often, whose mind stagnates and breathes unwholesome vapors, — idler and ease-taker, if, in reading of Mr. Clayton, your heart has not responded with interest to his action — if your own mind does not feel a stimulus to like things — say if it is not clear, that Mr. Clayton was wiser and happier in his good work, though it involved care and some sacrifice, than in the droning round of efforts to kill the passing time that marked his previous days?

XXVI.

A POOR SERMON, AND WHY.

"ORSE and worse." Mr. Hilton spoke with ill-concealed displeasure, as he stepped from the church door. "I've never listened to anything so dull and disconnected as the sermon preached this morning."

"Certainly our minister does not improve," was the discouraging response.

"Improve! Goodness! I should think not."

"He gave us some excellent discourses in the beginning — the best, in fact, ever preached in our church. But for some cause, he's been running down for a year past. In fact, he's not the man he was. I don't understand it."

"I do, then," said Mr. Hilton, the parishoner who

had opened the subject of complaint. "It lies just here — Mr. Orne has preached himself out. He's evidently a man of limited range, with a few good sermons, the utmost he can do. Having swept round his narrow circle of ideas, he has nothing further to give, and so goes plodding and stumbling along the way of prosy mediocrity."

"It may be so," was answered. "But I have read Mr. Orne differently. Every now and then, he flashes up in a way that indicates mental power and originality. Even in to-day's sermon, poor as it was, I noticed many choice things, but to most hearers they were probably lost through the deadness of utterance."

"They certainly were to me," returned Mr. Hilton.

"He does not seem to be at ease in his mind," remarked the other.

"I know nothing as to that. If a minister, who is supposed to dwell on the mountains of spiritual tranquility, is not at ease in his mind, who may hope to be?"

"Ministers are but men, and of like passions with the people."

"They are men, of course, and with like passions," said Mr. Hilton, "yet are supposed to live above the world, and to hold their passions under rule. Men who set up to be ministers should practise as well as preach, and show, by living example, the truth of doctrine. They must not only point to Heaven, but lead the way."

"I'm afraid," was replied, "that, as a general thing, we are inclined to look for too great perfection in our clergymen. To demand the highest Christian graces, though, like ourselves, they are burdened with hereditary evil, and struggling in the bonds of temptation. We have many excuses for our own shortcomings, but none for theirs."

"I can accept no excuse for Mr. Orne's shortcomings in the pulpit," returned Mr. Hilton.

"He has preached better. Contrast his trial sermon, with the stupid harangues now given; could anything be in more painful contrast? Either he has preached himself out, or don't care how his Sunday services are performed. In either case the fact is conclusive against him, and marks his unfitness for this parish. We ought to get rid of him. He does not suit us. He isn't the man for the place."

The two men had arrived at a point where their ways diverged, when they stopped long enough for Mr. Hilton to finish the last brief sentences, and then separated.

It was true as had been charged, that Mr. Orne's sermon, on that Sabbath morning, was a very dull performance, and it was true, also, that for some time he had been growing duller and heavier in the pulpit, only flashing up, occasionally, with his wonted fire. There was, of course, a cause for all this. Let us see if we can find it. Let us look in upon Mr. Hilton during the six days preceding the Sabbath on which he made this last unsatisfactory effort, and see if light can be found.

It was Monday morning, and there dwelt with Mr. Orne a troubled consciousness that his discourse on the preceding day had been sadly below its theme, and that he had neither watered his flock nor led them into green pastures.

"I *must* do better," he said to himself, with an effort to spur his mind into activity. "I must shake off this incubus." And he went resolutely to his study, where, after praying for light and strength, he sat down with his books and memorandums, and searched for an appropriate theme on which to write his next discourse. But he found it impossible to fix his thoughts on any subject long enough for a growth of ideas. Now he considered this text and pondered that, but his mind seemed as if dwelling in a closely sealed chamber, into which no light penetrated. He might think out some commonplaces, weak and trite, and throw them into dull sentences. But there had been enough of that. He wished to do better.

At last thought began to play, with some activity, around a certain passage of Scripture. A window seemed opening in his mind; rays of light streamed through, and he had glimpses of azure sky, and a world of beauty outside of his prison-house. Now his pulses beat quicker, and with exhilarant life. The old pleasure was coming back into his heart. He had passed to the world of ideas. Already sentences of stately form, full of thought, and glowing with heavenly ardor, were beginning to flow from his pen, when the door of his study opened softly, and his wife came in. He looked up at the intruder, as his eyes rested on her countenance, the windows of his prison-house closed, and all his mind was circumscribed and in darkness as before, for there was trouble in her countenance.

"Mr. Folwell has called again," she said, in a tone of discouragement that was infectious.

Mr. Orne experienced the sensation of a shock, followed by such a constriction of the chest that respiration became difficult.

"I shall have to see him, I suppose." And he shut the portfolio that lay on his table, put aside his pen, and rising, went down stairs, not with a quick, elastic step, but lagging and reluctant.

"Good morning, Mr. Folwell." He tried to greet his visitor cheerfully, but the effort failed.

"Good morning," was answered back, but in no gracious manner.

"Take a chair." Mr. Folwell sat down.

"You've called for that money." The voice failed a little.

"Yes, sir," very decidedly spoke Mr. Folwell.

"Well, I'm extremely sorry." The visitor's brows knitted, and his shut mouth grew harder. Mr. Orne hesitated in his speech, faltered, and then kept on. "But, indeed, sir, it is wholly out of my power to settle your bill to-day. I expected to receive the money long before this, but have been sadly disappointed."

Mr. Folwell put on a severe aspect.

"Will you fix a time on which I may certainly calculate on receiving my money?"

The minister had no resources beyond his small salary, the last quarterly payment of which had now been deferred over six weeks, during a greater part of which time he had been anxiously awaiting its receipt, in order to liquidate certain bills contracted for supplies without which his family would have suffered. Hurriedly weighing the chances of receiving, within a few days, the portion of salary due, and likewise determining to see the treasurer and ask for it, if not forthcoming, a thing he would avoid, if possible, Mr. Orne made answer:

"On Saturday, at the latest, you shall be paid."

"Very well, sir." Mr. Folwell arose, and buttoned

his coat to the last button with cold deliberation. "I will call on Saturday." And he bowed with a formal, impressive air, meant to say, "Don't forget your promise, sir, for most assuredly I shall not."

The minister bowed, almost meekly, in return, and the two men parted.

Back to his study crept Mr. Orne, stooping as though his shoulders were burdened. He sat down to the table again, opened his portfolio, lifted his pen, and commenced reading over the few paragraphs he had written on the next Sabbath's sermon. Twice, three times, he read them; but the sentences conveyed no living thoughts to his mind. They opened not the door to a world of ideas. He was in darkness and obscurity. Resolutely did he seek to follow out one suggestive word after another, recorded on the page before him; but just as he would seem to be ascending into the region of light, the cares of this world would pull at his garments, and drag him down into obscurity. He had promised to pay Mr. Folwell on Saturday. Would he be able to keep that promise? The intrusion of this question acted like a chill to his rising mental ardor, and sent it shivering back into torpor.

"It's of no use! I can't do anything on my sermon to-day," said the poor man, almost despairingly, as he shut his portfolio, and bowed his head upon the table.

After dwelling for some time on the embarrassing nature of his worldly affairs — embarrassing in part, through inadequacy of income; but, chiefly, because the payments on his salary were not made promptly when due — Mr. Orne resolved to see the treasurer of the church, and advise him of his pressing needs. A few words will make his case clear. On reaching this parish, after accepting a call, the expense of removal had nearly exhausted Mr. Orne's slender purse, and as no payment was made to him until the first quarter expired, he was, at that time, in debt for things absolutely needed in his family to amount of nearly half the money received. It seemed as if he could never make up this deficiency. At the end of every succeeding quarter he found himself in debt, and obliged to pay away nearly the whole of his slender income as soon as received. After a year or two, pewholders and subscribers to the fund for his support, grew careless in regard to payments, and it often happened that two, three, four and even six weeks elapsed, after Mr. Orne's salary was due, before the money came into his hands. Whenever this occurred, he would be worried by calls for settlements not in his power to make, and often hurt by the unfeeling words that disappointed creditors are sometimes wont to speak. He was a sensitive, honorable man; and debt brought his mind into bondage. He could never meet a person whom he owed, and feel unembarrassed. Since coming to this charge, he had lost a portion of that manly freedom so dear to most minds, and without which no clergyman can do justice, in preaching, to himself or congregation. No wonder that his people felt the inadequacy of his ministrations.

Acting on his purpose to see the treasurer, Mr. Orne lost no time in calling on this individual, for he felt that, having promised to pay Mr. Folwell on Saturday, he would not be able to write a line on his sermon until assured of having the means to keep his promise.

"You've been expecting to see me," said the treasurer, with a brief smile of welcome, as Mr. Orne entered his store. The minister grasped tightly the hand of his parishioner, forced an answering smile, but did not reply in words. The two men walked to the after part of the store, away from clerks and customers.

"I'm sorry to say, there isn't a cent in the treasury yet."

" Mr. Orne tried not to betray any disappointment — tried to feel calm — tried to bear up bravely.

"Will you receive anything during the week?" he asked, in a subdued voice.

"It is uncertain. I can't very well dun the people, you know."

"I wouldn't have you do that," said Mr. Orne, hardly knowing what he replied.

"Two or three of our subscribers are considerably in arrears," remarked the treasurer, "and it's mostly their fault that we're behind with your salary. There's Mr. Hilton, for instance, who hasn't paid in one cent for more than a year — and he's well off — if he, and some others just like him, would make their accounts square, like Christian men, I could pay you promptly at the end of each quarter. It's all wrong. But, what are we to do with such people, Mr. Orne? I wish you'd show them up in a sermon."

"I've promised a bill of twenty-five dollars on Saturday," said the minister, going to the heart of the matter. "Try and get me that sum, if possible. A minister, above all other men, should keep his engagements, for, if he does not, how can he preach of justice and judgment to any good purpose?"

"If the money comes in, Mr. Orne, you shall certainly have it; but don't depend, too entirely, on receiving it from me."

"If the money comes in! Was that an assurance strong enough to tranquilize the clergyman's mind? Could he return home, and get up a fine sermon for the next Sabbath on so vague a promise of the means for paying Mr. Folwell's debt on Saturday? There are men, who could have pushed even as disturbing an element as this aside, and risen above its influence into the regions of pure thought, but Mr. Orne was not of this number. He did not even look at texts, skeleton sermons, or memorandums of subjects again that day.

Men of a highly sensitive organization, are apt, when anything troubles them, to brood over it on going to bed at night, and in a half sleeping half waking state, lie for hours suffering a kind of mental torture that exhaust both mind and body. Such a night succeeded to this unsatisfactory Monday, and Mr. Orne wrestled with haunting shadows through all its lonely watches. A dull pain over his left eye, as he arose unrefreshed from his pillow on the next morning, gave warning of a lost day — and not only of a lost day, but of one doomed to intense suffering from nervous headache, which did not leave him until after succeeding midnight.

The day following one of these paroxysms of headache was always a day of exhaustion, in which rest and quiet were essential; and so Wednesday passed without the first line being written on his sermon. On Thursday, a funeral at eleven o'clock, five miles away, consumed his morning, and also his afternoon until three o'clock, when he arrived at home in no condition to think or write with any degree of clearness or vigor.

On Friday, with a kind of desperate energy, the minister sat down in his study, and endeavored to throw his mind into a discourse, the subject of which had been chosen as he lay in the calm moments that follow sleep when thought awakes with morning. But he had not written long, with conscious feebleness, before his mind perversely wandered aside, and imagination began to picture the meeting with Mr. Folwell, on the next morning.

"I must have this settled first," he said, at length, pushing his manuscript aside. "Under such a weight of doubt and uncertainty it is impossible to think clearly." And Mr. Orne took his hat and walked down to see the treasurer. On seeing him approach, the treasurer looked sober, and shook his head.

"Nothing in the treasury yet?" Mr. Orne forced a smile to his lips, and tried to look composed.

"Nothing," answered the treasurer.

"Any prospect for to-morrow?"

"I'm afraid not. Yesterday I saw Mr. Hilton, and asked him outright for his subscription. He was half offended, and said he had other use for his money just now."

"I'm sorry."

"So am I," said the treasurer.

"I don't know what I shall do. I promised Mr. Folwell that he should have his money to-morrow, and he'll be sure to call."

"It's too bad," said the treasurer, fretfully. "If

subscribers and pewholders are not more prompt in paying up their dues, I shall resign my office. I'm willing to keep the accounts, and disburse all moneys that come into my hands; but I can't act the part of a collector, and go about hunting up delinquents."

Mr. Orne lingered for a little while, vainly hoping that the treasurer would offer to advance the sum needed to make his promise good, and then went despondently home again. For an hour he wrote on his sermon, conscious all the while of giving forth common-place truths, in which dwelt no sympathetic life. Then anxious care obstructed all influx of ideas, and he arose and walked the floor of his study pondering the morrow's trouble.

"I must keep my promise," he said, bitterly, almost hopelessly. And so he went out to see if he could not borrow the sum needed. Now there were many of his parishioners who were able enough to lend, and many both able and willing. But to none of these did he feel free to go. So he applied to a single individual, who, however willing, was not able to lend him twenty-five dollars. This failure, on his first essay at borrowing, sent him home mortified and discouraged, and to compelled work on the discourse that must be ready for the next Sabbath. Night came, and it not one third done.

Saturday morning found the unhappy minister wholly

unprepared to meet his surely coming creditor. He went to his study after breakfast, but not to write on his sermon. That was impossible. He was walking the floor when his wife came in and said:

"Mr. Folwell is down stairs."

Sadly they looked into each other's eyes for a moment, and then Mr. Orne left the room.

"I am hurt and grieved, Mr. Folwell—"

A flush of angry impatience burned in the man's countenance.

"I am hurt and grieved, sir; but I am still without a single dollar through which to make good even a part of my promise," said the minister, helplessly.

Mr. Folwell tossed his head, and drew himself up in a superior way, remarking:

"A promise should always be kept. At least, so we men of the world think."

His tone was cutting. Mr. Orne shivered internally. He felt humiliated in person and in office.

"You said I should have the money to-day," added the creditor, taking a cruel pleasure in hurting the poor sufferer, who stood helpless and in shame before him. "I believed you on the word of a minister. And now you tell me that I can't have it. We men of the world hold our promise more sacred, but maybe we have too nice a sense of honor."

Mr. Orne did not answer. He was hurt too keenly by these thrusts.

"When shall I call again?" There was irony in Mr. Folwell's tones.

"I cannot fix another day," answered the minister, speaking without any sign of resentment. "When I receive the amount, I will bring it to you within half an hour after it comes into my hands."

"The parish owes you."

"Yes. I would have starved rather than take your goods without a prospect of paying for them. I saw our treasurer yesterday, and expected to receive from him the sum needed to make good my promise. He had no funds. What am I to do?"

"Preach to your people on common honesty!"

Mr. Folwell flung the sentence rudely into Mr. Orne's face, and then, as he turned away, said, in almost a sneering voice:

"Good morning!"

All the rest of that day, and until after eleven o'clock at night, the unhappy minister wrought at his sermon, wearily and without heart; and on the next morning preached it in a dull, cold way to an unresponsive audience, some of whom were growing tired of his poor performances, and beginning to think, as we have seen, that he was not the man for the place. And he was not. The people of that parish, too many of whom were of the Mr. Hilton type, needed a man of different mettle. One who, taking the text given by Mr. Folwell, would have startled their consciences by a sermon on common honesty.

There are a great many parishes in which the minister, like Mr. Orne, seems to have preached himself out, having lost vitality, range of thought, beauty and strength; and grown dull, self-absorbed, and almost indifferent, who goes plodding and stumbling along the way of prosy mediocrity. Take a hint my friend, if you belong to one of these parishes, from the case of Mr. Orne, and look a little more closely than you have done into the pecuniary condition of your minister; and if you are of the Mr. Hilton type, in the name of religion and humanity, pay up your subscription before finding fault with his preaching! Ministers are but men, and if you lay upon them anxious cares for food, and raiment, and humiliations in the face of those who may take pleasure in wounding them, how are they, thus weighted, to be swift and strong?

XXVII.

OLD GRIFFIN, THE USURER.

THERE was one thing that old Griffin, the usurer, loved better than money — one thing, and one only — his daughter. She was not beautiful, either in form or features. Through neglect in childhood, she had contracted a disease of the spine, which left a sad curvature. This obstructed free nervous action, and so the whole physical life became dwarfed. Her face was weasoned, and her form diminutive. She stooped forward, bending to the right; and one shoulder stood above the other. Of course, her movements were ungraceful.

For all this, everybody that knew Katy Griffin loved her. The sweetness of her temper, the kindness of her heart, the good will shown in benefits where it was fitting to bestow them — all these gave the impression of a soul that lived nearer to heaven than to earth.

One day, the angels lifted this beautiful soul out of its deformed earthly body, and bore it, clothed in an immortal body of spiritual substance like their own, upwards into heaven. There had been only slight warning of the change. Katy had drooped a little, but without complaining. Then she went to sleep, like a tired child, and the heart of the hard old man, her father — hard to the world, but soft to his child — was stricken with a sorrow beyond the power of healing.

The long cherished greed of money, which had grown into second nature, was not diminished by this event. Pain seemed to stimulate instead of weakening the passion. Old Griffin exacted from the weak and necessitous who came to him in their extremity, the largest discounts to which they would submit; often taking from poor men, forced by present needs to sell the notes of hand received in payment for work, at the rate of thirty, forty, or fifty per cent. per annum! All day long he sat in his office, like a great bloated spider, waiting for the flies that were sure to be entangled in his web; then he went back to his home, from which the light had gone out, and sat there in darkness and grief.

With the money taken by the old usurer from needy merchants, manufacturers and mechanics, he built a splendid monument over the grave of his child. Within the massive iron railing that enclosed this monument, seats were placed; late in the afternoon, after the day's business was over, you would find old Mr. Griffin, when the air was warm and the sky clear. Choicest flowers bloomed around the monument.

"*She* loved flowers." This was his answer to a stranger who, seeing him in the little enclosure one day, entered and stood by his side, saying, as the old man looked up:

"These flowers are very beautiful."

"*She* loved flowers."

"Your daughter," responded the stranger.

"Yes. She was never without them."

"You loved her very much," said the stranger.

"Loved her!" said the old man. "Love seems too common a word to express my feelings. Our language wants a new term."

"Everybody loved her," returned the stranger.

"Did you know her?" Mr. Griffin looked up at his companion curiously.

"I know those who both knew and loved her. A few times she has come in my way, and I felt her sphere like that of some blessed one."

"O, sir, she was an angel on the earth!" The old man spoke with a tremor of enthusiasm.

"And is now an angel in heaven."

"I believe it, sir. O, yes — I believe that. If she is not with the angels, and herself an angel, who shall hope to enter the Kingdom of Heaven?"

"Which is a kingdom of love and use," said the stranger.

"I don't know," replied Griffin, a dull shadow falling on his face — "I'm no theologian, and don't pretend to understand their phraseology. The talk of your pious people is generally Greek to me."

"Did Katy love herself?" asked the stranger.

"She was the most unselfish being I ever knew," promptly answered the father, with a flush of pride in his face.

"Always doing good, as she had opportunity."

"Yes, always."

"Do you think she comes to you often, now that she has laid off her earthly vesture?"

"I am sure of it," was answered. "Though my bodily eyes may be too dull to see her, yet love tells me that she is near."

"And she looks into your heart — knows what you feel and think — sees, by her more interior vision, away down into the secret places of your life."

Old Griffin's countenance changed. It became more thoughtful, and just a little troubled.

"In coming near to you now, she sees past all outward things. No feeling, no purpose, no quality of mind is hidden," continued the stranger. "Have you thought of this?"

The old man's head drooped upon his breast. His eyes rested on the ground. He made no answer.

"Let me relate to you a little incident," said the stranger. The old usurer raised his head.

"A poor, honest, hard-working mechanic had a sick child, whom he loved very much. Your child was no dearer to you than his child was to him. This poor mechanic had other children, and it taxed all his efforts, and took all his earnings to buy them plain food and clothing. The sick child needed many things not in the father's power to give. She needed to be taken out into the pure air — to have change, and cordials, and luxuries his slender purse might not afford.

"I met your angel-minded daughter in the chamber of this sick child, one day. She had brought some delicacies to tempt her appetite, and a bunch of flowers to refresh her senses. 'On Saturday,' said the child, warmth coming into her wan face, 'father is going with me to the sea-shore. The doctor says it will do me so much good. Father will take me down, and leave me there for a week. I shall be so happy! I never saw the sea. How grand it must look.'

"My heart went with the child in her journey to the sea-shore. I knew that both body and mind would receive a healthy influence. I wish you could have seen the pleasure that shone in your Katy's face, as she saw the joy of this poor sick child. 'I'm so glad you are going,' she said, taking her little hand. 'When you come back I will see you, and you must tell me all about the grand old ocean.'

"Well, sir, Saturday came, but the sick child did not see the ocean, nor get health from its cool and stimulating breezes. Why? Let me tell you. Her father, as I have said, was a poor man, who toiled hard for his money. It so happened, that he was doing work for a person who promised him pay as soon as the job was completed. He had to buy material with which to do the work, and for which he was to settle on receiving payment. The work amounted to little over seventy dollars, and the cost of the material was thirty-five. When the job was done, instead of receiving cash, as he had expected, the poor mechanic could only get a note of hand payable in four months. This would not have been a serious inconvenience, or loss, if the money could have been obtained thereon at legal interest; but there was no person known to the mechanic who would discount the note at any fair rate. The promise to the sick child was made in expectation of receiving this money when the work was done.

"Well, sir! The poor mechanic brought this note of hand to you. It was for seventy dollars, bear in mind. Common interest for the four months it had to run would be about one dollar and a half, counting in the grace days; but you cut off twenty dollars. 'I'll give fifty or nothing,' you said to the poor man. 'The maker hardly ever pays his notes. Ten chances to one but I lose by it in the end. In fact, I'd rather not have his paper.' And yet you were buying the same man's paper every day, and considered it good.

"Only fifteen dollars of profit was left to the poor man for two weeks of hard work. You took the rest! Of course, the sick, failing, longing child did not get the sea breezes. No — no. And she died a month later. I saw Katy standing, with tear filled eyes, looking upon the pale corpse. She had brought flowers to lay in the coffin. Of course, she knew nothing of your part in the tragedy. The grieving father would not wound her tender heart by even a hint at the miserable truth.

"But things are different now," continued the stranger. "Katy's inner eyes are opened. She does not come to you in the outside world of veils and shadowing curtains of flesh; but as soul comes to soul — spirit to spirit. If there is subterfuge in your mind, she sees it. If hard, grasping selfishness, that would take from a sick and dying child the very breath of life and coin it into gold — she sees that also. Can she love these? Nay, can she love him who admits and cherishes them? Ah, sir! If you would have this heavenly-minded child near you, you must love what she loves. If you would go to her when you die, you must set your heart on higher and purer things than treasure that moth corrupts."

The old man was stunned. He sat, with eyes cast down, still and statue-like. When he lifted his eyes, the stranger was not near. He had departed, with noiseless steps.

Next day a poor man came to the usurer. He had a note of sixty dollars.

"How much shall I take?" said the usurer to himself, as he looked greedily at the signature. It was on his lip to offer the poor man forty-five dollars for the note. But, a thought of Katy kept the sentence back. She seemed to be standing close beside him, observing all that he was thinking and doing.

"This is for work," he said to the man, speaking, as he felt, to two auditors — one visible and the other invisible.

"Yes, sir. It is for work."

"All for labor?"

"No, sir. At least half for material."

"Was there a good profit on the work?"

"No, sir. It hardly paid for day-labor."

"Ah! Is that so?" The usurer sat in a thoughtful way, holding the little piece of paper in his hand. More palpably present seemed Katy. "Is that so?" he repeated. "Then the case is slightly altered. You can't afford much discount."

"Every dollar taken from that note," said the poor man, "is so much lost from my hard earnings; so much bread taken from my children."

A brief struggle took place in the usurer's mind; then he filled up a check for fifty-eight dollars and sixty-three cents.

"I've charged only common interest," he said, as he gave the check.

"It is very kind in you, sir, very kind!" answered the poor man with feeling. "They said you'd take the hide off; but I knew it wasn't in the heart of one so full of riches as you are to rob a poor man's children. I'll put such slander back into the teeth of any one who utters it again in my presence." And the man went out.

"Was that right, Katy?" Almost aloud the old man said this, as if Katy were in bodily presence beside him. He felt the warmth of her approving smile — the sweetness of a new emotion, born of an act which had in it the germ of a higher and nobler life. Never before had he denied the lust of gain; never before conceded, except to his child, anything for another's good.

In all that day's business there was conflict. Greed of gold prompted to the usual exactions; but the ever-recurring thought of Katy, with the impression of her nearness, held him away from extortion, when the weak and needy came to him. On large commercial paper there were current "street rates" of discount, which, though usurious, he made without scruple. But when the artisan and the small manufacturer came, with their sober faces and small notes, the conscious presence of Katy restrained him. He dared not rob them as of old, lest the pure spirit he so loved should see it and depart from him.

And in the days that followed he could not go back to the old hard ways of grinding the needy whenever they were forced, through necessity, to seek his aid. Always the hand of Katy seemed on his hand, holding it back from cruel greed; always she seemed close by his side, observing his acts, and looking down into his heart. In time, new thoughts stirred, and new questions arose, in his mind. Glimpses of things higher than the mere sensual and corporeal were given to his unsealing eyes. He began to have a dim perception of the truth, that gold was not a satisfying element. That the more he gained the more he coveted.

One day, when the old passion for gain was strong upon him, he lost his usual sense of Katy's presence, and robbed a poor man, in pressing necessity, of twenty-five dollars — that being the excess of discount over what was legal on a note of one hundred and twenty-eight dollars. Scarcely had the man, with a sad, discouraged face, gone out from his office, when he became distinctly conscious that Katy was by his side. She had seen it all! This was the thought that flashed into his mind. Very still, he sat, oppressed with a feeling of guilt and shame. He had done this mean and selfish thing. Had taken the poor man's hard-earned profits, and added them to his bursting coffers; and angel-Katy had seen it all!

Pain and repentance were in his heart. Not so much for the act as for the dreaded consequences. Would not Katy go away from him in sorrow; because he was base, sordid and cruel?

"I will end all this!" he said, in a passion of fear, lest he should lose his child. "Dear Katy! do not leave me — do not go away. It was wrong — all wrong. I didn't reflect. It was the old bad way; but I will not go in it any more."

So he talked, almost crying, in a weak, quivering, half childish manner, wringing his hands.

"I will send him the twenty-five dollars. He shall

have it all back again." He went on talking aloud. And he opened his check book, filled up a check for the sum mentioned, and enclosing it in an envelope, wrote upon it the man's address.

"Here," he said, with a deep sigh of relief. "I've made restitution." And the old man felt easier in mind after that. Katy, as it seemed to him, drew closer. He almost felt her breath on his cheek — her light arms twining about his neck.

" Lay up treasure in heaven." Was that her voice? How palpably it struck on the sense of hearing, as if it had come by an outer instead of by an inner way. The old man started, half turning. What a flood of new and better thoughts came rushing into his mind.

" Gold perisheth in the using; but good abides for ever. Every good deed is a coin laid up in the treasury of heaven."

Somewhere, he had heard or read these sentences, and they had fixed themselves in memory. Now, the dust of years was swept off by some angel-hand, and he saw them as distinctly as if they were but just recorded.

So the work was going on in old Griffin's mind. Slowly — with small promise at the beginning — under many hindrances and obstructions. But, after awhile a small channel for a new life-current was cut into the hard rock of nature and habit, and a healthy stream began to flow therein with a perceptible current. At last the usurer gave up his calling. He said, "I have enough." Then there was a pause. His life seemed to stand still. There was an aching void in his heart. But, in a small silver thread, the new current flowed on, and there was a gradual deepening and widening of its channel.

Then his gold began to be a burden. He must use it in some way. He felt this impulse growing stronger and stronger. Katy's presence was still a palpable thing. He never lost the thought of her. What will she think ? How will it appear in her eyes ? Will she love me better for this ? So, ever to the lost but present one, he kept turning and turning; and this thought of her gradually led him, after ceasing in what was wrong, to the doing of good deeds.

Twenty years after Katy's death, the old man died. Many wet eyes saw him coffined; and many voices, burdened with feeling, were lifted in blessings on his name. The spirit of his departed child had led his feet heavenward, and we may have faith that, standing on the threshold of the city of God, the pearly gate opened, and he passed in to dwell in safety forever

XXVIII.

A SPUR IN THE SIDE.

THERE are men in whose side the spur has to be driven. Without it, they would never reach to half their possible speed; never accomplish anything worthy of their powers. Some men, like spirited horses, move freely to their work, under the impulse of an ever active will, while others suffer from the inertia of a sluggish temperament. There may be as much actual force in the latter as in the former, but the spur must be felt ere the sleeping energies will arouse themselves.

It is a sad necessity, this, for having a spur thrust into the side, but there are a great many of us to whom the world is indebted for a respectable amount of useful work, who would have accomplished very little if we had not felt the spur. People who look at our hurt sides pity us, and think the case hard — often say, that the world treats us with injustice; gets from us more than it gives. But He that considereth the sparrows, knoweth what is best. The smart is only for a season; but in the work done and the distance accomplished, there is a delight that overpays all.

My excellent friend, Mr. Garland, Rector of St. P———'s, presents a notable instance in point. He has what is known to be a poor parish. The salary is light, and the pay irregular as to times and amounts. Mr. Garland's family consists of seven members — himself, wife, four little children, and a domestic. This is the regular establishment for which provision has to be made. It rarely happens, however, that a month goes by without the addition of visitors from a distance — "Comers and stayers," as the old lady calls them, who take possession of the "best room," and sojourn pleasantly with the pastor and his family for indefinite periods, shorter or longer, as inclination or convenience prompts. The visiting element in my friend Mr. Garland's family, may be fairly set down as equal to the permanent addition of one member; so that he has eight mouths to feed.

Now, it so happens, that Mr. Garland is not gifted with economic intuitions. It is often said of him that "he doesn't know the use of money." "That may be," he remarked, good humoredly, when the saying was repeated to him, " because I see so little of it." It is true, however, that in the careful use of money his education is defective. Were his salary doubled, I question whether he would be any better off at the year's end than he is now.

A very uncomfortable life is that of the Rector, in many of its features, as you can imagine, and yet, it has its compensations and enjoyments, even under circumstances of discipline that some men would call purgatorial. In the matter of sermonizing, he is very unequal, sometimes he will drone along in a discussion that is pointless and lifeless, and sometimes he will send electric thrills of thought and emotion through his congregation, and seem like one inspired.

" I don't wonder that he is dull," said a friend of the pastor's, in answer to a complaining member, as they walked home from church on one of the stupid Sundays, as they were sometimes called. " The only wonder is that he can preach at all. Give him a better salary, and set him free from the perpetual dunnings of butchers and grocers, and he'll preach for you as well as the next. Can a man think and write with a dozen unpaid bills lying on the table before him? I trow not."

The complaining member was answered and silenced. If his last half year's subscription to the church fund had been paid, he might have had a word or two more to say. But, under the circumstances, he offered no further objection.

I enjoyed the Rector's society very much, and sought it on all fitting occasions. He was educated, liberal in sentiments, refined in character, genial as a companion, and highly gifted; but he was "weighted," as the "country parson" would say, with a sluggishness of temperament, that, when permitted to bear him down, left half his powers of mind inactive. It was only when the spur was in his side, that he sprung to his work with an outlay of full strength. The smart quickened his brain, and set all its fine machinery in motion. I happened to know that, during the week preceding the dull Sunday performance of which the parishioner complained, Mr. Garland had enjoyed unusual freedom from disturbing influences. The next week he was not so favored, however.

Monday morning found the Rector in not a very comfortable frame of mind. He knew that he had done badly on the day before, and that the congregation had gone home about as hungry for spiritual food as when they came to worship and receive instruction, but was unable to see how he could do better in future. Mind was dull and dark — there was no flashing of light through it — no palpitating consciousness of strength. It did not seem to him that he could ever write another sermon. A haunting sense of duty led him to search about, in a half-dead and alive way, for a subject suited to the state of his congregation. "I must do better on next Sabbath," he said, in a miserable self-upbraiding spirit, yet not rising out of his sluggish mental state. An hour or two spent in the effort to fix upon a subject, proved so fruitless, that he left his study, and was about leaving the parsonage for a walk or a visit, when the carrier met him at the door with a letter. It was from the editor of a semi-religious and literary periodical, and the contents were a brief reminder on the subject of an article he had promised; said article being one of a series for which he was to be paid.

The reception of this letter gave annoyance to Mr. Garland, instead of pleasure. The articles to be written were on subjects that not only required research and study, but mental effort, in the production, of no ordinary kind. It was because he was known to have ability for the work, that he had been selected. Two of the articles had already been furnished, and they were so able and exhaustive, that all who had read them were looking with interest to his completion of the series. This was the second reminder he had received, nearly two months having gone by since his last article made its appearance. Mr. Garland had gone back to his study on receiving the letter. After reading it, he sat down in a weak, almost helpless state of mind. There was no consciousness of strength for the giant's work demanded; and he shrunk with an instinct of weakness from the effort. Still, the work must be done — adequately or inadequately. He had undertaken its performance, and his promise, as to time, had already been broken. More than this, the money that would be forthcoming immediately on his transmission of the article, was due to parties who had more than once asked for payment. Here was incentive enough, you will say. And yet, the powers of my friend, the Rector, were not quickened into vigorous life. The spur was needed — the smarting side that would electrify the brain.

For an hour longer the Rector occupied his study, forcing himself to the task of gathering material for his third article; but he wrought coldly and sluggishly. He could not get interested in his work. Pushing, at last, his books and his papers aside, he was rising from his study table, and saying to himself — "It's of no use; I can't make anything out of this to-day." When there came a knock at the door. He opened it, and met an unwelcome face.

"Oh, Mr. Young!" he said, trying to smile; but the muscles would not go beyond gravity. "Walk in."

Mr. Young walked in with a solid tread and a cold, resolved manner.

"Take a chair, Mr. Young."

The visitor sat down; and the Rector, with heightening color, sat down, also. The two men looked at each other; one with a hard exacting expression, the other with timidity, shame, and helplessness.

"You know, of course, why I am here," said the former.

"I am sorry that there should exist a necessity for your calling," returned the Rector.

"So am I," was the blunt response. The visitor was drawing from his deep breast pocket, as he spoke, a large pocket book. From this he selected, with deliberate movement, a bill, and handing it to the Rector, said—

"I trust, for your own sake, that you will settle my account to-day. I have no wish to give you trouble, Mr. Garland, but as I've been put off, now, for over three months, I've made up my mind not to be bamboozled any longer."

The heel was heavy that struck a spur into my friend's side; and the pain that followed was sharp, thrilling along every nerve.

"It is impossible to do anything to-day," was replied, with a troubled air. "Impossible, Mr. Young."

The visitor's heavy brows contracted.

"Oh, very well," Mr. Young's countenance was threatening. He thrust the pocket book into its place, in an angry manner, and rose from his chair.

For a a few moments the Rector beat about in his mind helplessly. Then he said —

"The bill is twenty-five dollars."

"That is the amount, sir," answered the visitor.

"Can you wait, say ten days longer?"

"What can you do in ten days?" was asked in a cold, incredulous tone.

"Pay your bill, I hope."

"You hope!" The man shook his head.

"We are not certain of anything in this world," replied the Rector, regaining something of his lost dignity of manner. "It is for us to use the best means in our power; the result is with God. I have an article to write for a periodical, and will, on its completion and delivery, receive twenty-five dollars. The moment that sum comes into my hand, you shall have it. It will take two or three days to complete the article; and several days will elapse after sending it before I can receive the money. I think that I may safely say, that in ten days your bill will be settled."

"Oh, very well! Take your ten days," said Mr. Young, still with a rudeness of manner that hurt my friend. "If the money is forthcoming then, well; if not, I know my remedy. Good morning, sir."

As already remarked, the heel was heavy which struck the spur into the Rector's side on this occasion, and the accompanying pain sharp, thrilling along every nerve. He did not leave his study after his visitor retired, but sat down to his work, with every faculty stretched to the proper tension. Before night-fall he was well into the elaboration of his article, his mind acting with a clearness and vigor that made composition a delight. This was on Monday. By Wednesday evening it was finished, and I then had the pleasure of listening to his fine reading, with his soul alive in all the sentences, of one of the most splendid magazine papers he had yet given to the work for which he was a favorite contributor.

After this brilliant effort, made under the spur, my friend the Rector fell back into one of his sluggish states of mind, and there was danger of another stupid Sunday performance. He saw and felt this, but had not resolution enough to arouse himself and compel activity. Friday found him droning over a dull discourse, in which memory and not thought was present. On Saturday morning he took up, heavily, the burden he was trying to carry, and staggered along with it in a halting manner. Another stroke of the spur was needed, and the stroke was given. He had latent power enough; but it needed will and impuise. Once in motion, mind acted with singular strength and beauty, and so it acted now. The incident which gave impulse on this occasion, came as a consequence of the apparently inadequate support received in his office; but was dependent chiefly on his own lack of prudence and forethought in worldly matters. It was effective, however, and providentially permitted for a good end. A new theme was suggested to his mind, and all alive from sudden pain, he wrought upon it with vigor and rapidity, bringing forth a suggestive and useful sermon, equal to anything I had heard him deliver.

Mr. Garland understood his own case, and when I referred to the wide difference between the two discourses given on consecutive Sabbaths, answered — "It was the spur, my friend. I am a sluggish animal, and reach my best speed at the expense of pricked sides."

How many of us are like Mr. Garland, Rector of St. P——'s. It were better if we could give to our work, always, from a will impelled by love or duty, the full measure of power with which God has endowed us. Failing in this, it is better for the world, and better for ourselves, that life should be quickened by pain, and all our faculties thus stimulated to effort. Even though moving under compulsion, there is more delight in high mental activity than in droning half-work, or stupid idleness. And so even the pricked sides, against which we so often complain, are the result of merciful Providence; and better for us than the ease and freedom from care, trouble and misfortunes, so ardently longed for, but not given, lest they should curse our own lives, and rob the world of its claim on our ability to serve the common good.

XXIX.

A NEW WORK AND A NEW LIFE.

"OH, dear! Who can that be? As to seeing any one this morning, it is wholly out of the question!"

Mrs. Crawford arose, and going to the window, turned the venitian blind so as to look downward, and ascertain, if possible, who had rung the door bell. There was a lady on the step; but only a portion of a black silk dress being visible, Mrs. Crawford could make out the caller's identity.

"Mrs. Scofield," said the servant, a little while afterward.

"Mrs. Scofield!" In a tone of surprise, mingled with fretfulness.

"Yes, ma'am. She's in the parlor."

"O, dear! It's of no use, Bridget; I can't see any

body this morning. Tell her that I'm not at all well, and that she will have to excuse me."

The servant stood for a moment or two, in a hesitating way, as if waiting for the lady's mind to change.

"Tell her that I'm very sorry; but —"

Mrs. Crawford checked herself. Considerations not at first seen arose before her mind, and caused a change in her purpose.

"Say that I'll be down in a few minutes."

The servant retired with this message. In a dull, moody way, Mrs. Crawford went about effecting some changes in her dress, which occupied nearly ten minutes.

"I'm sorry to have kept you waiting," she said to her visitor, on entering the parlor. Her smile was kind enough, for she really liked Mrs. Scofield. But it soon faded out, giving place to an unhappy look.

"Are you not well?" asked Mrs. Scofield, noticing her sober aspect.

"I'm miserable," was the emphatic response. "Miserable! No other word so well expresses my condition." The dim ghost of a smile played about the lips of Mrs. Crawford for an instant, and then vanished.

Mrs. Scofield waited for something more explicit.

"The fact is, taking my experience, life is a wretched affair at best. I'm disheartened," added Mrs. Crawford.

"Disheartened about what?" asked the friend.

"Oh, about everything. All seems to be going wrong."

"I'm pained to hear you speak so, Mrs. Crawford. What particular thing is going wrong with you?"

"Well, there's the old standard trouble — servants. The bad ones torment, and the good ones leave you. I had a cook who was a perfect treasure. Meals always ready in time and well served. But, of course, she grew dissatisfied, though I humored and gave way to her in almost everything. Last week she left me, and we are now at the mercy of a raw Irish recruit, who doesn't know how to boil a potato. I shall send her flying to-morrow. With a husband as particular as mine is, you can guess at the annoyance to which I am subjected. Then again, my chambermaid is going away. She gave me notice yesterday. If I was right well, I wouldn't care so much. But, I'm not as I used to be — neither so strong to endure in mind or body. Little things, that didn't, in past times, disturb me at all, now set my nerves all in a tremor."

Poor Mrs. Crawford! She was the image of distress.

"Everything about me," she resumed, "is getting into disorder. My furniture is growing dingier day by day, just for want of thorough rubbing and attention, which you cannot get from servants, unless you stand over them all the while. It makes my heart sick! And if you follow them up, and insist on having things done your own way, they grumble or grow impertinent. It's terrible to live in this way! In fact, it's killing me by inches. If I was one of your don't-care, easy-go-lucky kind of people, who let things run at sixes and sevens, and have a jolly time of it with life, for all, it might be different. But I am not. I must have order and neatness around me, or I'm miserable!"

Mrs. Scofield in the pause that followed this complaint, said, with a certain sobriety of manner that was just shaded with reproof:

"These things are annoying, of course, Mrs. Crawford: but, when we compare them with what thousands, yea hundreds of thousands around us are now enduring, do they not fall into insignificance?"

Mrs. Crawford did not reply, and the friend went on.

"I have seen things during the past week that so rebuke me for complaint of life's petty cares and annoyances, as to make my cheeks burn with shame. Have you visited any of the hospitals?"

"O, no. My nerves would never stand that," quickly answered Mrs. Crawford.

"In the face of appealing pain and sickness, the nerves grow strong," said Mrs. Scofield. "My own heart failed me as I crossed the threshold on my first day's visit to the sick and wounded, and I was faint as I entered the wards. But interest and sympathy soon overcome weakness, and when I saw a pale, enduring face brighter at a kind word, I felt twice repaid for the effort it had cost me to go in. I have spent hours in the hospitals every day since then, and I have called this morning to ask you to go with me. There is something for us all to do."

"Oh, but indeed, Mrs. Scofield, I am not strong enough. What can I do?"

"A hundred things, if your heart is but willing. Come! I cannot accept your no. Put on your bonnet and shawl. If brave men fight for the protection of our homes, it is the least that loyal women can do, to care for them when sick or wounded. If you are not strong enough to bear the fatigue of a nurse in the wards, you can at least provide something for a sick, exhausted man, whose very life depends on a quality of nourishment not supplied by government. I appeal to you in the name of our country, in the name of humanity, and in the name of God!"

The appeal was successful. Mrs. Crawford, under the impulse excited, went with her friend to visit the government hospital, in which were over a thousand sick and wounded soldiers. Stretching away for hundreds of feet beyond the entrance door, she saw a double row of beds, most of them occupied. Her first impulse was to stop and turn back. It seemed impossible for her to go forward. How could she look this body of suffering, much of it unto death, in the face? Her heart shivered, and stood still for a moment.

"Indeed, Mrs. Scofield — " She caught the arm of her friend, and drew back; but the sentence remained unfinished, for a pair of appealing eyes were resting on hers, and holding her as by a sudden spell. Just to the right of where she was standing, and a little in advance, was a bed, on which a wounded soldier was lying. He was but a stripling; a boy scarcely in his nineteenth year.

Naturally, Mrs. Crawford had a tender heart. With the sentence unfinished on her lips, she moved to the bed on which the boy was lying, and stooping over him, laid her hand softly on his forehead.

"Are you very sick?" she asked, uttering the first question that came to her thought.

"I've been wounded," replied the young soldier, trying to smile and look brave. But Mrs. Crawford noticed a quiver about his mouth.

"Wounded! Oh — I'm sorry! Not badly, I hope." Mrs. Crawford sat down in a chair that stood near the bedside.

"A ball struck me in the hip, and shattered the bone. I don't know that I shall ever get well."

The momentary weakness had departed, and the boy spoke firmly, though a little sadly.

"Are you in much pain?" asked Mrs. Crawford.

"Not now, ma'am."

"When were you wounded?"

"I was in all the battles before Richmond. On the third day I was struck and left lying on the field when our army moved away. The rebels carried me to Richmond, and put me in prison with a great many other wounded men, numbers of whom died. I suffered dreadfully. One of their doctors examined my wound, and took out the ball. He said I'd never get well. Then they sent us back, under a flag of truce, and I was brought here."

"How long was it from the time you were wounded until you reached here?" asked Mrs. Crawford.

"Over three weeks, ma'am."

"And nothing done for you in all that time?"

"Not much, ma'am. The doctors had their hands full everywhere. In Richmond they had more than they could do to attend to their own wounded. No one seemed to care what we suffered, or whether we lived or died. Poor wounded fellows — some horribly mangled — were thrown down, anywhere, on the hard floor, and not even straw given them to lie on. At least it was so in our prison. A great many never saw the face of a doctor, and died for want of attention. They did all they could for us, when we got back within our own lines; but men get hardened after being for awhile among the wounded. I was lifted about very roughly sometimes, in being taken on and off the boat, and hurt a great deal. But I'm very comfortable here."

And as the soldier uttered his last sentence in a tone of satisfaction, a smile played around his lips.

"To what regiment do you belong?" asked the lady.

"To the — Massachusetts, Company B. I went from Springfield."

"Have you friends there?"

"Yes. My mother and sister live in Springfield."

"Do they know that you are wounded?"

"If my name was in the paper they have seen it. But I can't say whether it was published or not."

"You haven't heard from them since the battle in which you were hurt?"

"No."

"How long have you been in this hospital?"

"Only three days."

"And they don't know that you are here?"

"No ma'am. I'm not strong enough to write yet."

"Shall I write for you?"

The boy's face lit up — gratitude beamed from his eyes.

"If it would not be too much trouble."

Mrs. Crawford took a pencil and card from her pocket, and wrote down the name of the soldier's mother.

"Shall I tell her all that you have told me? Let her know just how badly you are wounded?"

The young soldier shut his eyes, and remained silent for some moments.

"No, that would distress her too much," he said, with a thoughtful air. "It will be bad enough for her to know that I am wounded. Tell her, if you please, that I am getting on very well here, and hope to be on my feet again before a long time. Say that a ball passed through my leg; but don't speak of my shattered hip. They've taken out two pieces of bone since I came here, and maybe I'll get all right. Anyhow, it won't do any good to let her know the worst on the offstart."

"Perhaps she will come on to see you?" said Mrs. Crawford.

Tears sprung to the poor fellow's eyes; but he wiped them off quickly. He did not reply to the suggestion; but it was plain to see with what joy he would have welcomed her.

"I will write the letter as soon as I go home. And

now, is there anything I can do to make you more comfortable; anything that I can get for you?"

A wishful look came into the lad's eyes. It was his only reply. Mrs. Crawford saw it, and half comprehending its significance, said:

"Don't feel backward. If I can do anything for you, the act will give me pleasure. How is your appetite?"

"Not very good."

One hand was lying outside the bed covering. Mrs. Crawford touched it.

"You have some fever," she said.

"That's the reason, perhaps, why — "

The sick lad checked himself, and a slight flush came into his face.

"Speak out freely. Just think that I'm your mother, and tell me what you want." All the heart of Mrs. Crawford was going out toward the wounded boy.

"You're very good and kind, ma'am," he answered, "and you won't think me foolish or unreasonable. But, you see, a lady yesterday brought some grapes to a poor, sick fellow, across there, and, as he ate them, I longed so for just two or three that I almost cried. It wasn't right I know. But, indeed, ma'am, I couldn't help it. And ever since I've been longing for some grapes. It's the fever, maybe."

A NEW WORK, AND A NEW LIFE.

"You shall have them!" said Mrs. Crawford, rising quickly; and away she went, under the impulse of pity and kindness, leaving the hospital without thinking of her friend Mrs. Scofield, and hurrying off to a fruit store, where she bought a pound of juicy, hot-house grapes. She was back again in less than half an hour.

"They will not hurt him?" she said to the nurse in charge of the bed on which the wounded soldier lay.

"You may give him half-a-dozen now," replied the nurse.

"Oh, they are so good!" exclaimed the lad, as he crushed the luscious fruit in his mouth, and swallowed the refreshing juice. His eyes sparkled, and smiles ran over his face.

"It was very kind of you, and I shall never forget it as long as I live." His countenance beamed with pleasure and gratitude.

"Keep the rest for him," said Mrs. Crawford, handing what remained of the grapes to the nurse in attendance on that part of the ward. For nearly an hour longer she remained with the young soldier, listening to his account of life in camp and on the battle-field, so deeply interested that she scarcely noted the passage of time. Then, promising to see him again on the next day, she went home to write about him to his mother.

How different was Mrs. Crawford's state of mind on

reaching home, and entering the room where only a little while before she sat brooding miserably over life's petty troubles. How mean and insignificant appears these troubles now! She felt rebuked and humiliated.

When Mr. Crawford left his wife in the morning, she was in one of her fretful, gloomy, self-tormenting states, which had led him to say, as he went out of the breakfast-room:

"Don't wait dinner for me. I shall dine down town to-day."

This was happening two or three times every week, notwithstanding Mr. Crawford had long ago became disgusted with eating-house fare. But he preferred the restaurant to home, with its fretfulness and gloom.

Thought and feeling with Mrs. Crawford were all setting in a new current. Her sympathies were deeply excited. During the brief period she remained in the hospital her eyes had taken in enough to stir human nature to its profoundest depth. Chiefly she had given herself to the boy-soldier, and let her first efforts expend themselves for him, because the work came like ripe fruit into her hand. But, even as she sat writing of him to his mother, other countenances besides that of the lad, and other cases that called for help in silent pleadings, arose before her, and filled her heart with compassionate desires.

It was a little past six o'clock when Mr. Crawford came home. The thermometer of his feeling gradually went down as he approached his pleasant dwelling — pleasant so far as all things external were concerned. He remembered the gloomy face he had left in the morning, and experience gave him no fair promise of finding smiles instead of shadow. He opened the door quietly and went in. His step along the hall was not strong and confident, like that of a man within his own castle, and glad to be there; but in part restrained, and scarcely arousing an echo.

"Is that you, Edward?" The voice came down from the first landing. There was a quality of feeling in the tones that made Mr. Crawford leap with surprise and pleasure. He saw the old beauty in his wife's face; the old rippling light in her eyes; the old, sweet tenderness about her mouth — and new-born love made the offering of a kiss spontaneous.

"You cannot guess where I have been, Edward." Mrs. Crawford had drawn her arm within her husband's. The smile faded gently from her countenance, over which a tender seriousness spread itself.

"Where?" He inquired with interest.

"To one of the hospitals."

"Why Helen!" He might well look surprised.

"And I'm going to-morrow again — and every day."

Mrs. Crawford spoke with animation. "I saw a poor wounded boy there, not over eighteen or nineteen, and I've been writing for him to his mother. His bright eyes and almost girlish, but suffering face, were like a spell on me when I went in, and sat down to talk with him. His hands were hot, and his mouth feverish — poor boy! his hip had been shattered by a ball — and when I asked him if there was anything I could get for him, he said, hesitatingly, that he had been longing for some grapes. I went out immediately, and bought him some Black Hamburgs. Oh, if you could have seen his eager, delighted face as he crushed them in his mouth! It repaid me a thousand fold."

Mr. Crawford quietly drew out his pocket-book, and taking therefrom a roll of bank bills, said, with considerable feeling, as he handed them to his wife:

"As your heart prompts, so do, Helen. I am with you in this noble duty. Give all your days to the work, and let home take care of itself. We have surfeited ourselves with the good things of this world, until they have commenced palling on the taste. Now, let us find a new life in gift and ministration."

And a new life was born in the heart of Mrs. Crawford. Daily she spent hours among the sick and wounded, or in the preparation of things needed for their restoration and comfort; and though a witness of suffering in terrible forms, and of almost daily deaths, she yet maintained a calm and cheerful exterior, and filled the home her fretful, dissatisfied spirit had once overshadowed with gloom, with an all-pervading sunshine.

It was remarkable how quickly all trouble with servants came to an end. There was a new spirit in the mistress, which pervaded every part of her household, making duty and obedience a pleasure, and not a task. Instead of perpetual hindrances, there soon became manifest a common desire to act with Mrs. Crawford in all her cheerfully expressed wishes, leading to unity and harmony, which are the hand-maidens of peace.

XXX.

CARE-WORN.

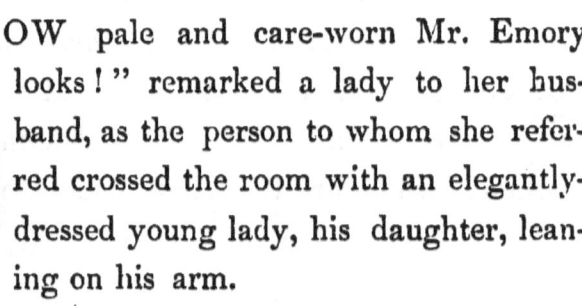"How pale and care-worn Mr. Emory looks!" remarked a lady to her husband, as the person to whom she referred crossed the room with an elegantly-dressed young lady, his daughter, leaning on his arm.

"No wonder," was replied. - "Mr. Emory has enough to make him look pale and care-worn."

"Has anything happened in his family?" The lady turned curiously toward her husband.

"I believe not."

"What is wrong, then?"

"Much; as witness the troubled look that rests always on his face when it is in repose. A peaceful mind never records itself in such an expression. I am glad to see him among us for a few days. He needs the change and mental recreation — needs them a great deal more than nine out of ten who are here. But he can not stay long enough to receive any permanent benefit. Wife and daughters will remain; he must speed back to the city."

" Why ? "

" Business."

" Yes, that is the word with men. They worship business with the blind devotion of idolators. Every thing is sacrificed to business."

" Why ? "

The husband's face was serious. His wife did not answer the question.

" I will tell you. It is chiefly because men, in our day, try to do more business than they are able to manage. They are anxious to secure large returns in a brief time."

" Men should be wiser and more prudent," was responded. " Common sense should teach them a better way."

" I grant you this. But there are influences at work with almost every man that too frequently prove stronger than prudence or common sense."

" What are they ? "

" Social pride."

" Has that any thing to do with Mr. Emory's care-worn face ? "

"Every thing. Mr. Emory possessed a business, ten years ago, which, if rightly managed, would have made him to-day an independent man in the world, instead of one almost harrassed to death. It is the old story. His family must occupy a certain position in society. They must go with the fashionable crowd. There must be a fine house and costly furniture; dress and show; costly emulations. All these things require money. It is easy to sink a few thousands of dollars every year in home extravagances, and have nothing very satisfactory to show for it at the end. Two thousand dollars a year for ten years make the handsome sum of twenty thousand dollars; and I'm very sure that, without the abridgement of a single comfort or the removal of a single element of rational enjoyment, at least that large amount of money could have been saved by the family of Mr. Emory during the period mentioned. What then?"

"Mr. Emory would have been just twenty thousand dollars better off than he is to-day," said the lady. "So much richer, but whether any the less a pale, care-worn devotee of business is open to a doubt. This business, it strikes me, is a kind of mental disease."

"Only in a few cases," was replied. "In Mr. Emory's case, as I happen to know, necessity, and not impulse, is the law of force. I saw him ten days ago, and the interview left a painful impression on my mind. We are personally intimate enough to talk freely together. I said to him,

"'Are you going to the sea-shore this year?'

"He shrugged his shoulders and smiled faintly. It was the ghost of a smile, dying almost as soon as born. 'Can't get away, even if I could afford it.'

"'Why can't you get away?' I asked.

"He reached his hand for his bill-book, and opening to the month of August, pointed to half a page of entries, which my practical eyes very well understood. 'Foots six thousand and upward,' said he, significantly.

"'You have the funds in bank, or to come in during the month,' I remarked.

"'Not five hundred in bank,' he answered, looking painfully concerned, 'nor a thousand beyond on which any certain calculation is to be made. So you see I shall have to be on hand all the time, just to work and scheme in the direction of money-raising. Heaven only knows how I am to get through! As for business, I might shut my store for a month and not be any the worse off.'

"'I wish, from my heart,' said I, speaking from a kind impulse toward Mr. Emory, who is a true man, 'that you had twenty thousand dollars in bank.'

"'I should be the happiest man alive!' he answered,

with a sudden light flashing over his face. How quickly that light receded! How sad the face its fleeting radiance left behind!

"Now two thousand dollars a year for ten years, saved in expenses which have not increased the happiness of his family one iota, would have given to Mr. Emory a large sum of money. With that in possession, I doubt if his face would be so pale and care-worn as you see it to-day. Visions of bankruptcy, of commercial dishonors, and of home desolations, the bare thought of which almost drive men to madness, would not haunt his waking reveries and midnight dreams. I see no reasonable hope for a safe deliverance out of his troubles. As his expenses went on eating into the life of his business, and payments became, in consequence, hard to meet, Mr. Emory increased his trade by forced means, not always safe — buying more largely, and selling to a wider range of customers, with less of scruple in regard to their standing, until he found himself in deep waters, and in danger. Since that time I am afraid it is growing worse with him instead of better. There is only one remedy, if its application be not already too late."

"What?"

"It is said that a knowledge of our disease is more than half the cure. This means that in a removal of discovered causes effects must cease. Mr. Emory's only hope lies in a reduction of his home expenses. If these go on, exhausting him more and more, ruin is inevitable."

"It will be a hard thing for his gay daughters to step down from their advance position," said the wife.

"Better for them to step down than to fall down. Down I am sure they will have to come, and that before a very long time. We shall hardly find them here in the next watering season."

A young lady, unobserved by the speakers, had been sitting in a window recess close enough to hear every word. She leaned and listened in an attitude of deep interest, her face flushing and palling by turns.

"Isn't that one of Mr. Emory's daughters?" said the lady to her husband, as the person referred to arose and crossed the long parlor.

"I believe so," was answered.

"It can't be possible that she heard your remarks about her father?"

"They were not meant for her ears; but if they have found their way there, well. I can not say that I regret their utterance."

"I'm sorry," said the lady. "Poor girl! How hurt and mortified she must be."

"All of her pain and mortification will be light in comparison to what her father suffers daily and hourly," was replied. "If she have any true love for him, she will now seek to lighten rather than increase his burdens."

The person of whom they spoke, Mr. Emory's second daughter, after leaving the public parlor, fled up stairs like one escaping from pursuit. On gaining her own room, she shut and locked the door — then sat down with her hands across her breast, pale-cheeked and panting. The aspect of her countenance was that of one oppressed by sudden terror.

Agnes loved her father purely and tenderly. She had not failed to observe the cloud which was gradually settling upon his life, nor the pale, care-worn face that looked in upon their home at the close of each recurring day. As Mr. Emory never referred to his business in the family circle, the true cause of this remained completely hidden. Not the remotest suspicion thereof had, up to this time, reached her apprehension. Suddenly a veil was drawn aside, and she stood in pain and fear, looking at the undisguised reality of her father's true position.

What could Agnes Emory do? Young, inexperienced, inefficient, through defective education, she felt her weakness, and for a time wept in conscious helplessness.

"Agnes!" It was her mother's voice.

The weeping girl endeavored to staunch her tears, but in vain. Her face was flooded as she opened the door.

"Why, Agnes, my child! what has happened?" said Mrs. Emory, in surprise.

Agnes tried to answer, but sobs came in the place of words. At length, as the turbulence of feeling began to abate, she said, with tears still falling over her face,

"Won't you ask father to come here?"

"Yes, dear. But why not tell me about your trouble first?"

"I'll tell you all about it. Oh, ask him to come, mother; and bring Emma and Alice."

In a few minutes Mr. Emory came hurriedly to Agnes's room, followed by his wife and other daughters. Already Agnes had been able to dry her tears; but her face was colorless.

Tenderly, almost pityingly, she looked up at her father, and seizing one of his hands in both of hers, held it tightly against her breast, saying, as she did so,

"Oh, father, if we had only known what was troubling you!"

"Troubling me!" answered Mr. Emory in astonishment, as he held Agnes a little way from him and gazed at her wonderingly.

"Yes, father, you've been troubled a long time. I've

seen it, and we've all seen it. You come home and sit silent all the evening. You have grown pale and thin. You look often so care-worn. And instead of helping you, we have only laid heavier burdens on your shoulders."

"What *does* the girl mean!" exclaimed Mrs. Emory, in a half-reproving voice.

"Come, sit down, dear, we must have all this explained," said the father, leading Agnes to a chair, and taking one beside her. "You say that I've been troubled?"

"Isn't it so, father?" Agnes raised again her brimming eyes to her father's face.

"This is a world of trouble, my child, and all must take a share," he answered evasively.

"Our share has been very light, and yours very heavy," was the prompt reply; "and now there must be a change. We must take off some of the burdens that weigh down your stooping shoulders. Oh, father! why did you not let us share them long and long ago? Did you doubt our willingness? did you question our love?"

"I am bewildered, my child," said Mr. Emory, his voice growing unsteady. "It is true that I am troubled — that my burdens are heavy; but from what source have you received information in regard to them? Speak out plainly, Agnes."

And she did speak plainly, relating, almost word for word, the conversation we have given.

"Is this all true, Edward?" said Mrs. Emory, as Agnes ceased speaking. Her voice was sad, but not weak. She had drawn near to her husband, and now stood with her hand resting firmly upon him.

"All true," was gloomily answered.

There fell upon the group of father, mother and daughters, a deep silence, in which heart-beatings were nearly audible.

"We have no right to be here," said the eldest daughter breaking the silence. "Let us go home to day."

"In the next hour, if a train starts," responded Agnes.

"Why did you let us come? Oh, father, it was so wrong — so wrong!"

And the youngest of the group laid her face down, weeping, on her father's shoulder.

"I meant to have spared you this," said the brave, enduring man, with an irrepressible emotion. "I trusted that all would come out right. I struggled hard to maintain myself, so that no shadow might darken my home. But I fear that all has been in vain. The weight lies too heavily upon me, and if not lightened in some way I must sink."

"You shall not sink, father, if we can bear you up,"

answered Agnes, bravely. "Let us go home to-day; and when we get home tell us everything about your business, so that we can understand just what duty requires. I'm sure we will all be of one heart and mind. If we are living too expensively, let us go down lower and take a humbler position. With what I heard just now ringing in my ears, I shall not have a moment's peace of mind until we retire from the public gaze."

"We are of one mind," said all. And with one mind they acted, starting for the city on that very day.

The change that followed was thorough, reaching to every department of their home life. In a brave and self-denying spirit wife and daughters rallied to the rescue. Watches, jewelry, surplus furniture, pictures, and articles of simple ornament, were sold, and the money, which reached the sum of nearly two thousand dollars, returned to the business from which it should never have been taken. Their large and handsome dwelling was exchanged for a cheap and modest home. One servant only was retained — three had been required — and the cost of living, under a system of the most rigid economy, reduced from between three and four thousand dollars a year to a ratio of about twelve hundred.

A new hope sprung to light in the heart of Mr. Emory. The money received for the sale of surplus furniture and articles of mere ornament came to his hand just in time to save him from protest, and carried him over a difficult place where he would inevitably have fallen. He felt that his ship was lightened; that she was answering more steadily to the helm, and bearing up to the wind. "Courage!" he said to himself. "I shall yet come out safely."

If the home to which Mr. Emory returned after each day's hard battle was humbler, the face he brought was not so care-worn. A cheerful light shone oftener in the eyes that were always sad before. He did not sit silent and withdrawn from the home circle as once, brooding over the dark and doubtful future, but read and talked through the evening hours with his wife and children, giving and receiving strength. Had the daughters lost more than was gained by the withdrawal from gay circles, and denial of pride and social ambition? Had duty been all a burden? Not so; duty is never all a burden. If it be sometimes hard and rough, there is always a sweet kernel at the centre. They were, in their seclusion and patient service, happier than before, and growing into a stronger, purer, and truer life. As for Mr. Emory, an almost despairing struggle with fortune had been changed for a hopeful one. Confidence took the place of doubt. He began to feel, under the lighter burdens that rested upon him, a more elastic and vigorous condition of mind. He was clearer-seeing and more sagacious in business. There was a lifting up of the darkness along the black horizon, and a promise of the coming dawn.

"Father is very late to-night," said Agnes, looking up at her mother, who entered the room where she sat with some needle-work in her hands. It was the evening of New Year's Day.

As she spoke, the father's well-known tread was heard in the passage.

"Oh, there he is now!" And Agnes laid aside her work, moving to meet her father as he ascended the stairs.

"How late you are!" she said, as she bent forward to receive the kiss that now almost always accompanied his return.

"It is late," replied Mr. Emory; "but I could not leave the store until I had completed some calculations I had in hand." His face was cheerful — more cheerful than it had yet been; radiant, in fact, with smiles.

"The work must have been satisfactory," said Mrs. Emory, "judging from the pleasant state of mind in which it has left you."

"It was satisfactory," replied Mr. Emory, with emphasis. "For two or three days we have been taking an account of stock, and to-day has been spent in closing the account and getting at the result. I am happy to say that it is more encouraging than was anticipated. Six months ago bankruptcy stared me in the face, and I saw no means of escape. Now I think the danger past. If I had been left standing alone, I must have fallen; but, wife and children sustaining me, strength came in the hour of exhaustion. All is safe now, I trust; safe for the present, and safe for the future. Our home is not so large nor so luxurious as it was on last New Year's Day; but then it rested on a sandy foundation, and the storm was gathering which, had it burst over us, would have left all in ruins. Now, solid earth and rock are beneath our house, and I do not shudder in fear of the rising tempest. Is it not far better with us than then? Are we not happier, though humbler?"

"Happier a thousand-fold!" said Agnes, as she drew an arm fondly around her father. "We speak of it to each other every day, and wonder at our former blindness and folly. To see smiles in the care-worn face of our father again — to hear him speak cheerfully and hopefully — to know that we have helped to lift burdens from his shoulders that were crushing him down — these are our rich reward!"

"And mine in having such children!" replied Mr. Emory, with feeling. "In every home, if rightly ordered, lie all the elements of happiness; and, thank God! we have found them at last. I was at fault in not taking you long ago into my counsels. How much of pain and peril might have been saved! But the night is past, and we bless the morning!"

And so might the morning break in thousands of homes over which shadows rest, if wives and daughters were wholly trusted, and made to comprehend the real struggle with fortune in which husbands and fathers are engaged. Thousands of pale, care-worn faces would grow warm and cheerful; and thousands of stooping shoulders, lightened of crushing burdens, grow erect.

Wives and daughters, ponder these things! Husbands and fathers, take them into your counsels!

XXXI.

SERVICE, NOT LOVE.

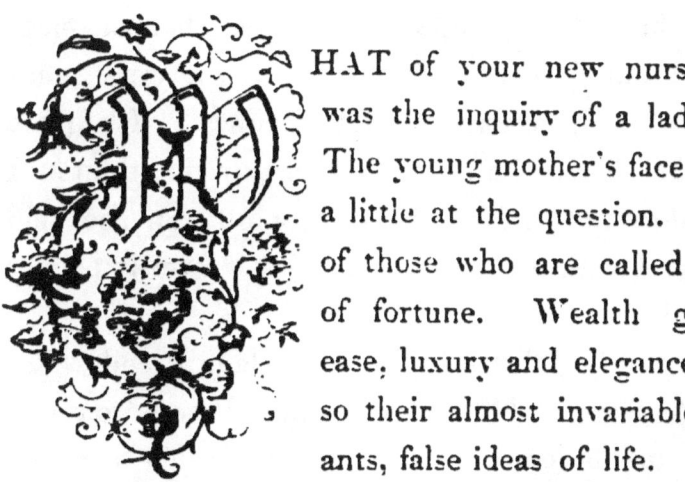HAT of your new nurse, Ida?" was the inquiry of a lady friend. The young mother's face changed a little at the question. She was of those who are called favorites of fortune. Wealth gave her ease, luxury and elegance, and also their almost invariable attendants, false ideas of life. Because poorer people were obliged to be useful and industrious, service of any kind was felt to have in it something degrading.

"She does not give entire satisfaction," added the friend, before Ida had time to reply. Her face had given the answer.

"No, far from it."

"What is the fault?"

"There's no heart in her," said the young mother.

"You mean that she doesn't seem to have any heart in her work."

"Yes, that's just what I mean. She handles the baby as if he were a senseless doll instead of the dear, sweet, precious thing that he is. She's as cold as an icicle."

"Isn't she kind and careful with the baby!"

"Yes, she's kind enough. I don't see that she neglects him; but she does everything as if she were a machine. So cold, so formal, so mechanical. It's mere duty-work. There isn't a bit of heart in anything. I can't understand it, Mrs. Nelson. How can she help gushing over with love and tenderness? I verily believe her devoid of feeling.

"I can testify differently," said the lady friend. Rachel has feelings, and they are warm. It was from seeing their exhibition, that I recommended her as nurse. At home she has a baby-brother and I knew that with him she is lavish of her love."

Ida's countenance showed some perplexity. She did not clearly comprehend the case. If Rachel had any warmth of feeling whatever, why was it not called forth by that loveliest babe her eyes had ever looked upon?

"For all I have seen of her," she replied, "I should say that she had no well springs of emotion in her nature."

"Such well springs are in all hearts, Ida," said the friend. "But they do not flow at the touch of every hand. Rachel has no personal interest in your baby. She is a nurse for hire. A hard necessity, as she no doubt considers it, forces her away from the care of an infant around whom love has twined a thousand delicate fibres that draw upon her heart; and she is compelled to give to your baby the care she yearns to lavish on the darling at home. She will be faithful to her duty; but she has no love to spare. So I read the case, Ida. Love is not bought nor sold. For hire you may get hands, but not hearts."

This was, to Ida, altogether a new and very unsatisfactory statement of the case. That it involved the truth, she could not help perceiving.

"The service," she answered, "in which there is no heart must, in the nature of things, be defective at some point. Duty work is always hard work, and the conscience which impels it must sometimes sleep."

"Undoubtedly."

Ida mused for some moments.

"And yet, Mrs. Nelson," she resumed, "I cannot but feel, that, in so sweet a babe as mine, the very sphere of his innocence must draw towards it a gush of tender feeling, unless the heart is very cold and selfish. Love should take the place of conscience."

"Would it, think you, in your case, Ida?"

"In my case! I do not see your meaning. How in my case?"

"Can you think out of yourself?"

"How, out of myself?"

"Realize conditions in life wholly different from those which actually exist."

"In my own case?"

"Yes."

"Perhaps I might, if the effort were made."

"Then, imagine such a change of circumstances as would require you to separate yourself from Francis, and become the nurse of another babe — just as pure and sweet; but not your own."

"You shock me, Mrs. Nelson! I can't imagine such a thing," said Ida.

"It is because you have imagined it, in a degree, that you are shocked," was the friend's reply. "Come up, bravely, Ida, to a fuller realization of the condition I have suggested. When you have done so, you will be able to understand Rachel — not before."

"I understood just now, that the babe she left at home was only a brother."

"True; yet was it born into her love, and dwelt in her heart with almost the fullness of delight that a mother knows. Thought and affection will be ever returning to the dearer babe she has left, even while the head of your darling, in all its sweetness and innocence, lies pillowed against her bosom. It is not that her heart is cold, Ida. But it is scarcely large enough for both these little ones. Now, go with me, in imagination. Misfortune has come, like a blighting wind, and the sheltering vine that shaded you from noontide heats is leafless and dead. The walls of your palace have been shaken to their foundations, and you go forth, weeping, to seek, in the wide, wide world, another and a poorer home. Nay, worse than all this, he who has kept even the summer airs from touching you too roughly, is taken away, and you are alone with your babe — alone, helpless and friendless. Such things have been, Ida; and such things will continue to be. Think, now, of leaving your own babe to the care of a sister, or a stranger, while you, for hire, take another babe to your arms, ministering to its wants, and giving it the tender services your heart is yearning to bestow upon your own. How much heart, think you, Ida, would there be in this work? Duty might be well done — the native kindness of your disposition might compel attentions — but, if love were also demanded, the requirement would be too great."

The friend ceased, and the young mother sat for some time in sober thought. She realized most vividly condition which had been pictured, and her heart shuddered at the distinct impression.

"What then?" she asked looking up, at length, with a shadow of a new consciousness in her eyes.

"What then? Many things are involved, Ida. We must not hope to get heart-service for hire, nor forget that love has its own world and its own precious things. We have our own world of precious things, our own idols, our own lares and penates, and so have others. That self-giving heroism which we think so beautiful is never bought nor sold, comes not through solicitation nor hire, but springs up in the soul under the inspiration of free and noble impulses, and makes life glowing and beautiful. Rachel is tender, and loving and true, but you can command her only on the plane of your agreement. She takes of you money, and pays you back in formal service. She will be patient and dutiful, but while her heart is with her baby brother, it cannot be more than dutiful under its new relation. Could your heart be more than this, Ida?"

"I think not. I am sure not." Ida's thoughts were busy with new suggestions. "I wish that I had known of this before," she said, with manifest concern.

"Why?"

"I might have done some things differently. The fact is, Mrs. Nelson, we are not so much inclined as we should be to give our domestics, and persons in humble circumstances, credit for the possession of like passions with ourselves. Rachel has been with me over two weeks, and only once during that time has she been home."

"Only once!"

"That is all."

"Has she not asked to go?"

"Yes, several times; but I could not spare her from the baby."

There followed a silence of several moments. Mrs. Nelson hesitated to utter the strong sentences that were in her mind. Ida arose, and crossing the room, rang a bell. To a servant who answered the call, she said:

"I want Rachel."

Rachel soon appeared with the baby in her arms. Her manner was, as Ida had alleged, cold, almost mechanical. There was a dreamy absence in her face, a dull abstraction in her eyes. Seeing Mrs. Nelson, who recognized and spoke to her kindly, a faint smile played about her lips. But it faded quickly.

"Give me the baby," said the mother, holding out her arms. The baby almost leaped to her loving breast, and murmured, in softest tones, its pleasure. Rachel, on relinquishing her charge, stood cold and passive.

"Would you like to go home for two or three hours, Rachel?" said Ida.

Her face lighted instantly. The statue-like frame seemed to quiver with feeling.

"O, yes, ma'am, very much," she answered, in an eager, fluttering voice.

"I think I can spare you, Rachel. Baby will be good. Don't stay later than six o'clock."

"Thank you, ma'am." The girl turned quickly away to hide the tears that were springing to her eyes; not, however, before they were seen by Ida and her friend.

"Do you think her cold and unfeeling? an icicle?" said Mrs. Nelson.

Ida shook her head, as she answered:

"No, my friend, neither cold nor unfeeling, but with a woman's heart beating, full-pulsed, in her bosom. What a new world you have opened to me, Mrs. Nelson! I can hardly understand myself. It is plain to me as noon-day, now, that love, before it gives itself to an object, must find something of its own therein. It is too free an element to be bought or sold. Our money will not acquire it."

"And for this reason, Ida, a mother's arms should oftenest be around her babe; a mother's bosom oftenest pillow its head. No other heart can feel the love you bear your infant — no other heart comprehend its gracious sweetness. Loving it so tenderly, should you not give yourself to your child, in all the fullness of your life; letting others share the precious charge only in the degree that health and social obligations may require. Should you not be its chief nurse? and Rachel the assistant? The possession of wealth, and the ability thence to pay for service, cannot absolve you of duty. A true mother will be to her babe what no other living mortal can; for its life has sprung from her life, and there is an interior communication between them, by virtue of this consanguinity and likeness of soul, which cannot possibly exist between the child and another. Be much with your babe, then, Ida. If the nurse is cold and unsympathetic, don't leave him, for any long period, in so chilly an atmosphere; but into the garden of his tender mind, now ready for planting, sow good seeds with your own hands — lest an enemy plant tares — and let him dwell much in the sunshine of your love, so that these seeds may find a quick vitality."

"I thank you, my friend," said Ida. "You have spoken plainly but truly. Your words have wrought conviction. I cannot buy love for my babe; and so must keep him nearer to my own heart. Precious darling!"

XXXII.

A RIFT IN THE CLOUD.

ANDREW LEE came home at evening from the shop where he had worked all day, tired, and out of spirits; came home to his wife, who was also tired and out of spirits.

"A smiling wife, and a cheerful home — what a paradise it would be!" said Andrew to himself, as he turned his eyes from the clouded face of Mrs. Lee, and sat down, with knitted brows, and a moody aspect.

Not a word was spoken by either. Mrs. Lee was getting supper, and she moved about with a weary step.

"Come," she said at last, with a side glance at her husband.

There was invitation in the word only, none in the voice of Mrs. Lee.

Andrew arose and went to the table. He was tempted to speak an angry word, but controlled himself, and kept silence. He could find no fault with the chop, nor the sweet home-made bread, nor the fragrant tea. They would have cheered his inward man, if there had only been a gleam of sunshine on the face of his wife. He noticed that she did not eat.

"Are you not well, Mary?" The words were on his lips, but he did not utter them, for the face of his wife looked so repellant, that he feared an irritating reply. And so, in moody silence, the twain sat together until Andrew had finished his supper. As he pushed his chair back, his wife arose, and commenced clearing off the table.

"This is purgatory!" said Lee to himself, as he commenced walking the floor of their little breakfast room, with his hands thrust desperately away down into his trousers pockets, and his chin almost touching his breast.

After removing all the dishes, and taking them into the kitchen, Mrs. Lee spread a green cover on the table, and placing a fresh-trimmed lamp thereon, went out, and shut the door after her, leaving her husband alone with his unpleasant feelings. He took a long deep breath as she did so, paused in his walk, stood still for some moments, and then drawing a paper from his pocket, sat down by the table, opened the sheet, and commenced reading. Singularly enough the words upon which his eyes rested were, "Praise your wife." They rather tended to increase the disturbance of mind from which he was suffering.

"I should like to find some occasion for praising mine." How quickly his thoughts expressed that ill-natured sentiment. But his eyes were on the page before him, and he read on.

"Praise your wife, man; for pity's sake, give her a little encouragement; it won't hurt her."

Andrew Lee raised his eyes from the paper, and muttered, "Oh, yes. That's all very well. Praise is cheap enough. But praise her for what? For being sullen, and making your home the most disagreeable place in the world?" His eye fell again to the paper.

She has made your home comfortable, your hearth bright and shining, your food agreeable; for pity's sake, tell her you thank her, if nothing more. She don't expect it; it will make her eyes open wider than they have for ten years; but it will do her good for all that, and you too."

It seemed to Andrew as if this sentence was written just for him, and just for the occasion. It was the complete answer to his question, "Praise her for what?" and he felt it also as a rebuke. He read no further, for thought came too busy, and in a new direction.

Memory was convicting him of injustice toward his wife. She had always made his home as comfortable for him as hands could make it, and had he offered the light return of praise or commendation? Had he ever told her of the satisfaction he had known, or the comfort experienced? He was not able to recall the time or the occasion. As he thought thus, Mrs. Lee came in from the kitchen, and taking her work-basket from a closet, placed it on the table, and sitting down, without speaking, began to sew. Mr. Lee glanced almost stealthily at the work in her hands, and saw that it was the bosom of a shirt, which she was stitching neatly. He knew that it was for him that she was at work.

"Praise your wife." The words were before the eyes of his mind, and he could not look away from them. But he was not ready for this yet. He still felt moody and unforgiving. The expression of his wife's face he interpreted to mean ill-nature, and with ill-nature, he had no patience. His eyes fell upon the newspaper that lay spread out before him, and he read the sentence:

"A kind, cheerful word, spoken in a gloomy home, is like the rift in a cloud that lets the sunshine through."

Lee struggled with himself a while longer. His own ill-nature had to be conquered first; his moody, accusing spirit had to be subdued. But he was coming right, and at last got right, as to will. Next came the question as to how he should begin. He thought of many things to say, yet feared to say them, lest his wife should meet his advances with a cold rebuff. At last, leaning towards her, and taking hold of the linen bosom upon which she was at work, he said, in a voice carefully modulated with kindness,

"You are doing that work very beautifully, Mary."

Mrs. Lee made no reply. But her husband did not fail to observe that she lost, almost instantly, that rigid erectness with which she had been sitting, nor that the motion of her needle hand ceased.

"My shirts are better made, and whiter than those of any other man in our shop," said Lee, encouraged to go on.

"Are they?" Mrs. Lee's voice was low, and had in it a slight huskiness. She did not turn her face, but her husband saw that she leaned a little towards him. He had broken through the ice of reserve, and all was easy now. His hand was among the clouds, and a few feeble rays were already struggling through the rift it had made.

"Yes Mary," he answered, softly; "and I've heard it said more than once, what a good wife Andrew Lee must have."

Mrs. Lee turned her face towards her husband. There was light in it, and light in her eye. But there was something in the expression of the countenance that a little puzzled him.

"Do you think so?" she asked, quite soberly.

"What a question!" ejaculated Andrew Lee, starting up, and going around to the side of the table where his wife was sitting. "What a question, Mary!" he repeated, as he stood before her.

"Do you?" It was all she said.

"Yes, darling," was his warmly-spoken answer, and he stooped down and kissed her. "How strange that you should ask me such a question!"

"If you would only tell me so now and then, Andrew, it would do me good." And Mrs. Lee arose, and leaning her face against the manly breast of her husband, stood and wept.

What a strong light broke in upon the mind of Andrew Lee. He had never given to his faithful wife even the small reward of praise for all the loving interest she had manifested daily, until doubt of his love had entered her soul, and made the light around her thick darkness. No wonder that her face grew clouded, nor that what he considered moodiness and ill-nature took possession of her spirit.

"You are good and true, Mary. My own dear wife.

I am proud of you — I love you — and my first desire is for your happiness. Oh, if I could always see your face in sunshine, my home would be the dearest place on earth."

"How precious to me are your words of love and praise, Andrew," said Mrs. Lee smiling up through her tears into his face. "With them in my ears, my heart can never lie in shadow."

How easy had been the work for Andrew Lee. He had swept his hand across the cloudy horizon of his home, and now the bright sunshine was streaming down, and flooding that home with joy and beauty.

XXXIII.

SABLES.

ANE!"

The young lady thus addressed, slightly turned her head, but did not respond in words.

"Did you hear me, Jane?"

"Certainly; I'm not hard of hearing," was answered, in a very undutiful way, considering the relation which existed between the two — that of mother and daughter.

"I want my needle book. You will find it in the upper drawer of my bureau."

Instead of doing what her mother desired, Jane arose, her manner showing great indifference, and crossing the apartment, gave the bell a quick jerk.

"I didn't ask you to ring for Ellen," said Mrs. Dunlap, showing considerable irritation. "My request was for you to get my needle book."

And the vexed mother got up hastily, and went out to do the little errand for herself. The servant a moment after came in.

"Did you ring, Miss Jane?"

"Mother wants you, I believe."

"Where is she?"

"Over in her room."

The young lady spoke in a very ungracious way.

Ellen, who had a weary, overtasked look, ascended another flight of stairs, and met Mrs. Dunlap at the door of her room.

"Did you want me, Ma'am?"

"No, Ellen;" her tone was kind.

"I thought you rung for me?" said the girl.

"It was a mistake, Ellen; and I'm sorry you were brought all the way up here for nothing, tired as you are."

The girl returned to her work, and Mrs. Dunlap to the sitting-room.

"I don't know what you keep servants for, if you don't make them wait on you," said Jane.

"When I want their services, I will call upon them," replied the mother, with some severity of manner. "And, hereafter, let it be understood that no servant is to be called for me, unless I ask to have it done."

Jane tossed her head in a way so like contempt, that

Mrs. Danlap was able, only by an effort, to keep back words of angry reproof. But experience had taught her that nothing of good for her vain, proud, self-willed child, was to be gained in angry contention. And so, with tears of sadness and vexation dimming her eyes, she bent her head low over the work upon which she was engaged.

Mr. Edwin Dunlap, the husband and father, was present, but during the occurrence of this little scene had not spoken a word, nor seemed to heed what was passing. The sofa upon which he sat stood at one end of the room, and he was removed from the lights. Neither his wife nor daughter noticed the depressed, abstracted manner which a close observer would have marked as indicative of some unusual trouble.

"Father!" The idle girl leaned back in the rocking chair that held her almost useless person, and turned her head partly around towards the sofa on which her father was sitting.

He did not answer.

"Father! Do you hear me?"

"Yes; what is it?" The voice of Mr. Dunlap was neither clear nor steady.

"Can't I have sables this winter? I've set my heart on it. I saw a muff and tippet to-day, for two hundred and fifty dollars, that are superb. Just what I want, and must have."

Mr. Dunlap did not reply, and so his daughter came again to the charge.

"You say yes, of course. When shall I get them? To-morrow?"

He was still silent.

"Very well. Silence gives consent. I'll call at the store to-morrow morning, and get the money. I knew you would let me have them. Oh, but they are elegant! The handsomest set I have seen this season."

And the young lady rocked herself with an air of the most perfect self-satisfaction.

But her father had not said a word. There was something in his manner that caused Mrs. Dunlap to let her hands fall in her lap, and look towards him with an expression of concern on her face. He had again relapsed into the state of abstraction from which the remarks of his daughter had aroused him, and now sat with his chin almost touching his breast. What was the picture in his mind? We will make an effort to reproduce it.

A small room, the floor covered with a poor quality of striped carpet — walls not even papered. A cherry breakfast table; four Windsor chairs; a pair of brass candlesticks on the mantle-piece; and figured paper blinds at the windows. This is nearly a complete schedule of the furniture. The inmates are himself and young wife. He was just returned from his day's work as porter in a large drug store. The leaves of the cherry breakfast table are spread open, and the top covered with a snowy table cloth, made white by the hands of his wife. The same hands have prepared their evening meal; and though the tea service is scant and plain, yet love and hope are smiling above their humble board, as they sit together, and talk of the coming future.

That was the picture! But it faded soon, though while it remained distinct, it was vivid as life itself. Poor, industrious, frugal, self-reliant, Mr. Dunlap and his wife had started in the world just twenty years before. Step by step had they ascended the ladder of fortune, until they stood high up among their fellows.

Like pictures in a kaleidoscope, life-scene after life-scene came and went, each showing some marked change in their external condition, until wealth and luxury crowned their toil and self-denial.

Mr. Dunlap had been naturally proud of his success in life; and we will not wonder that, from the eminence upon which he stood, he sometimes looked down with feelings of self-confidence and self-congratulation.

But to-night self-confidence and self-reliance were gone. He had built his fortune on what seemed an immovable foundation. But it proved to be one of sand, yielding with strange and frightful suddenness, and letting the beautiful edifice he had erected with such care and labor, sink into hopeless ruin.

Sables, at two hundred and fifty dollars! No wonder the unhappy man, in whose mind the certainty of his ruin, as a merchant, was gaining more palpable form every moment, did not reply. And no wonder the indolence and pride of his indulged and spoiled child, intruding at the moment, sent memory back to wipe the dust from pictures of the long ago.

Was she better than they were? Better than the faithful wife, her mother, who had walked in patient, humble industry by his side in the Spring-time of life? Even in his deep trouble of mind, the thought disturbed, and almost angered Mr. Dunlap. Not the incident of this evening alone, so far as Jane was concerned, now fretted him; but many incidents which intruded themselves like unwelcome guests, involving such false ideas of life, and such miserable pride and vanity, that he turned, half loathing, from the mental image of his child.

"If riches come at a price like this, then wealth is a curse instead of a blessing!"

The thought seemed scarcely his own, as he gave it involuntary mental utterance. Yet almost strange to say, the fearful image of misfortune, which had glared in the face of Mr. Dunlap, lost some of its repulsive features.

"The stern discipline of misfortune, I have heard it said, is always salutary."

How timely came the suggestion. It was an hour of pain and darkness; and yet the hand, as of an angel, was among the clouds.

"Jane." It was the voice of Mrs. Dunlap, that broke the silence of the apartment.

"Well, what's wanted?"

Jane was awakened from a dream of vanity and triumph. She was, already, in imagination, wearing the sables, and eclipsing certain young ladies whose pride she wished to humble. They had only mink, or martin at best, and she would hurt their eyes with sables.

"Jane, I wish you would go up to the large closet in the third story passage, and bring me a small bundle, tied with a piece of red cord, which lies on the top shelf."

"I'll ring for Ellen, if you desire it?" answered Jane, without moving.

"When I ask you to ring for a servant, you can do so," said Mrs. Dunlap, with unconcealed displeasure.

"I don't know what you have servants for, if you don't make them wait on you," retorted Jane sharply.

Mr. Dunlap turned his ear and listened.

"I wish *you* to get me the bundle," said Mrs. Dunlap. She spoke firmly.

"If there were no servants in the house, it would be fair enough to call on me to run up and down stairs," replied Jane, in increasing ill-nature. "But, as it is, you ask more than is reasonable; I'm not a waiter!"

This was more than Mr. Dunlap could bear. For weeks he had felt the storms of adverse circumstances bearing upon him with a steadily increasing violence; and with all the coolness of a brave commander, he had kept his eyes at the point of danger, and striven with unwearied skill to pass the reefs and currents amidst which his bark was struggling. But the events of that day had shown him that skill, courage, and toil were of no avail. The keel of his goodly vessel was already jarring among the breakers, and there was no human power that could save her from destruction. Our merchant was no coward. In his way up, he had striven hard, but gained mental stamina in the struggle after fortune. And now, when fortune was ebbing away like a swiftly receding tide, he did not shudder like a weakling. What if his ship were among the breakers? Life was yet safe. And something might yet be recovered after the hull went to pieces in the storm. And so, he was already nerving himself for the worst.

The last remark of his daughter was more, we have said, than Mr. Dunlap could bear. It had not been his intention to make known to his family, for a day or two yet, the painful trials that too surely awaited them. But this little scene excited a new train of thought, and he determined to speak out with a plainness that would leave no room for misapprehension. And so he rose from the sofa, and passed slowly towards the centre of the room. Both Mrs. Dunlap and Jane looked up into his face, and both half started with surprise at its paleness and strange expression.

"Sables? Did I hear aright, Jane?" Mr. Dunlap looked at his daughter in a wild kind of way. There was something in his voice that sent a shiver along her nerves.

"Yes, Sables," she answered, trying to speak in a firm and decided tone.

"You shall have them; and they shall be dark as midnight!"

Oh, with what a startling tone of bitterness were the words uttered.

The face of Jane grew pale, and the busy hands of her mother fell motionless in her lap.

"Yes, you shall have sables; but of another kind than those about which you have been so vainly dreaming. Sables for the heart — not for the idle hands and dainty shoulders."

Mr. Dunlap paused in his speech. Already he was conscious of having betrayed himself too far — of having commenced the announcement of approaching misfortune in a wrong and unmanly way.

"Oh, Edwin! What does this mean?" And the faithful, loving, strong-hearted wife, who had walked ever erect by his side, whether the sun shone or the rain fell, sprung forward from her chair, and grasping his arms, looked eagerly in his disturbed face.

Mr. Dunlap was a man of quick self-control. Only a moment or two of resolute repression was required to calm the turbulence of feeling which had been awakened.

"Sit down again," he said, in an even tone; and, as he spoke, he drew his wife towards the sofa from which he had a few moments before arisen. "Jane," he added, turning towards his bewildered daughter, over whose white cheeks the tears were already beginning to fall, "sit down by your mother; I have something to say that deeply concerns you both."

Then Mr. Dunlap took a chair, and drawing it in front of the sofa, sat down. There was a brief struggle for entire self-possession, and then the man was restored to himself.

"Margaret!" There was a tenderness in the tones of Mr. Dunlap's voice that stirred emotions long quiet in the bosom of his wife. "Margaret, as I sat here tonight, a picture of our little home — the first in which we lived together — came up from my memory, and stood before my eyes, with the distinctness of life itself. It looked poor and humble; but, Margaret, there was a sunny warmth in its atmosphere. We were happy — very happy in that little home. Have we been happier since?"

Mrs. Dunlap leaned over towards her husband, and looked with earnest inquiry into his face. His question was strange — his manner strange — his expression strange.

"Say, Margaret — wife — have we been happier since?"

"Happier? What do you mean, Edwin? Why do you ask the question?"

"Because I want it answered in your heart! Think! Have we been happier since?"

"We were very happy then, my husband."

"Though poor!"

"Yes."

"Poor, and toilers for our daily bread. Unknown — unnoticed — and yet happy!"

"And what of it, my husband? What of it?" asked Mrs. Dunlap, with a flushing face. "Speak out plainly! You frighten me by this strange mystery!"

Mr. Dunlap smiled. With him the bitterness of the trial had already passed. He was now calm and self-possessed.

"If we were happy once, though poor, can we not be poor and happy again?"

"Edwin! Husband!" Mrs. Dunlap's face turned suddenly white. "If anything has gone wrong with you, speak out plainly. Do you not know me?"

"Yes, Margaret, I know *you*." Then, after a slight pause: "Things *have* gone wrong. The storm that swept so many ships upon a lee shore, and among the breakers, did not spare mine. I strove hard to bring her safely into port, but strove in vain. She is even now going rapidly to pieces, and we shall save scarcely a timber from the wreck."

"My husband! Has it come to this!" And Mrs. Dunlap laid her head, weeping, upon his breast.

"We have life, Margaret, unsullied hearts, and hope still left. Courage!"

"If you can bear up, Edwin, with the pressure of this great calamity upon you, I have no cause of despondency. I did not think of myself, but you. Oh, to have the hard accumulations of your life-time swept away by a single wave! It is terrible, dear husband!

Trust in me; lean upon me; ask of me all things, and my heart will spring to meet your wishes. Oh, if you can but endure the trial bravely, it will have few sufferings for me!"

A wild tempest of weeping burst now from the daughter.

"Jane;" Mrs. Dunlap turned to her child. But Jane, without replying, arose and went from the room. A silence of some moments succeeded her departure. Then, Mr. Dunlap said:

"The ordeal will be a sad one for our proud, indolent child. My heart aches for her. But the discipline cannot fail of good result. We cannot save her from the consequences of misfortune."

"We ought not to save her if we could," answered the mother; "for there are better qualities in her nature, which new relations in life may develope. Wealth has been a snare to her feet, as it has been a snare to the feet of thousands. She has grown up in an atmosphere that has poisoned her blood. Hereafter, she will breathe a pure air; and I trust to its renovating influences."

"Poor child!" said Mr. Dunlap. "I spoke to her in too great bitterness — with too sharp irony. Alas! her sables will be darker than she dreamed."

The mother's hopeful prophecy showed earlier signs of fulfillment than she had anticipated. A short period of time only had elapsed, after Jane had left the apartment, before she returned again. Her face was pale, but not distressed; her eyes were red with weeping, yet were they not sad eyes, for the light of love was in them. She paused a moment at the door, looking wistfully at her parents, and then came forward with quick, eager steps.

"Dear Father!" she said, as she paused before them, "let me stand, also, by your side in this day of trouble!"

A thrill went through the frame of Mr. Dunlap, and springing up, he caught Jane in his arms, and hugged her to his heart almost wildly. Then holding her from him, and looking into her face fondly, he said:

"If fortune left so precious a jewel in the bottom of the cup she had drugged with bitterness, she gave blessing instead of cursing. Dear child! Upon the darkness of misfortune, light has arisen."

And now the strong man wept like a woman.

"To-morrow" came; but it did not bring the sables for Jane Dunlap. No, not even for her heart; for a new light had arisen there — a light so warm and radiant that it dispelled gloom from all the chambers of her mind; and not from hers alone, but from those of her parents also. They were happier in misfortune, than they had been in the sunshine of prosperity; for that only played over the delusive surface of their lives. But now, the sun of love, breaking suddenly through the rent clouds, made their hearts warm and fruitful.

THE END.

www.ingramcontent.com/pod-product-compliance
Lightning Source LLC
Chambersburg PA
CBHW021942240426
43668CB00037B/487